KARATE

AIKIDO, JU-JITSU AND JUDO

KARATE
AIKIDO, JU-JITSU AND JUDO

FAY GOODMAN

LORENZ BOOKS

This edition is published by Lorenz Books, an imprint of
Anness Publishing Ltd, 108 Great Russell Street, London WC1B 3NA
www.annesspublishing.com; info@anness.com
twitter: @Anness_Books

If you like the images in this book and would like to investigate using
them for publishing, promotions or advertising, please visit our website
www.practicalpictures.com for more information.

Publisher: Joanna Lorenz
Designer: Lisa Tai
Photographer: Mike James
Production Controller: Pirong Wang

A CIP catalogue record for this book is available from
the British Library.

Previously published as part of a larger volume,
The Ultimate Book of Martial Arts

THANK YOU

To those who have been kind – thank you
To those who have believed – I am grateful
To those who are sincere – you are deep in my thoughts
So let us never despair
When all appears against us
And the evil ones try to take our heart and soul
For those of you who have believed and never faltered
This is what living is made worthwhile for – I thank you

Fay Goodman

PUBLISHER'S NOTE

The author and publishers have made every effort to ensure
that all instructions contained within this book are accurate
and safe, and cannot accept liability for any resulting injury,
damage or loss to persons or property, however it may arise.
If you do have any special needs or problems, consult your
doctor or another health professional. This book cannot
replace medical consultation and should be used in
conjunction with professional advice. You should not
attempt martial arts without training from a properly
qualified practitioner.

CONTENTS

INTRODUCTION	6	**AIKIDO**	48	**JUDO**	112
		History and philosophy	50	History and philosophy	114
KARATE	8	Clothing and equipment	54	Clothing and equipment	118
History and philosophy	10	Etiquette	55	Etiquette	119
WADO RYU	14	Exercises	56	Exercises	120
History and philosophy	14	Techniques	66	Techniques	122
Clothing and equipment	16	Cooling-down exercises	78		
Etiquette	18			**INDEX**	128
Exercises	20	**JU-JITSU**	80		
Techniques	22	History and philosophy	82		
SHOTOKAN	34	Clothing and equipment	85		
History and philosophy	34	Etiquette	87		
Clothing and equipment	36	Exercises	88		
Etiquette	37	Techniques	92		
Exercises	38				
Techniques	40				

INTRODUCTION

It has long been known that a trained focus on mind and body can contribute greatly to a sense of well-being, so it is not surprising that more and more people are turning to the disciplines of the martial arts as a way of alleviating the tension and stress that are endemic in today's society. There are millions of martial arts practitioners all over the world. Through the disciplines these arts impose, men, women and children of all ages and abilities are actively involved in learning how to improve their awareness, health, fitness, confidence and their ability to protect themselves.

Much harm has come from the popular perception – learned largely from movies and fictional television dramas – that martial arts are concerned with violence and general mayhem. Anyone who becomes involved with the martial arts soon learns that the aggressive, brutish perception people have of these disciplines could not be further from the truth. Inherent in their teaching are the guiding principles of respect, courtesy and self-discipline.

In fact, most skilled martial arts practitioners are less likely to initiate or become involved in physical aggression than non-practitioners, preferring instead to remove themselves from a potentially violent situation. An aggressive approach is discouraged, both in training and real-life situations. Thus the martial arts serve to emphasize the development of respect, discipline and understanding. Rather than fighting other people, the martial arts

A young girl demonstrating the skill and precision required in karate. Good instruction is vital when learning a martial art at any age.

encourage us to fight the enemy within in an effort to become better people. Combine this attitude with the inner strength one gains from the training, and the rewards to be gleaned are peace of mind and a richer, more rounded quality of life.

The aim of this book is to give you an insight into a selection of martial arts commonly practised around the world today. Within the chapters you will find a brief overview of each martial art's history and philosophy and the essential clothing and equipment needed in order to participate. Etiquette, warm-up exercises and basic techniques are also included, as well as an insight into some of the weaponry that is traditionally used. Some of the techniques included here are for demonstration purposes only, in order to give you an idea as to what the chosen art has to offer in terms of stances, postures and the use of weapons, if any.

While some of the chapters give step-by-step instruction on how to practise some of the basic moves of the chosen discipline, there can be no substitute for learning from a professionally recognized, experienced and highly skilled teacher who will instruct and assist you in the development of your chosen art. The competitive element has a further part to play – indeed for many people the possibility of participation provides the motivation for training. However, it is important that you train in a safe environment, that you

The essence of judo is the utilization of your opponent's body weight as well as your own.

are aware of emergency procedures in case of accidents, and that you have proper insurance cover.

If you are a more experienced martial arts practitioner this book may introduce you to disciplines that you have not yet explored. It is very common for practitioners to study more than one art – the chief difficulty usually lies in deciding which others would be the most beneficial. The wide-ranging view given here of what each discipline has to offer, including the philosophies, skills and an appreciation of the benefits to be gained, should assist you in making the best decision.

Each discipline is covered in detail, including important warm-up exercises, the most popular and the more advanced moves. We also learn something of the teachers throughout the ages and their contribution to the skills we can enjoy today. The exciting world of martial arts has many doors, and in the words of one famous Chinese proverb: "Teachers open the door but we must walk through by ourselves".

The martial arts represent many ancient traditions and this book is an invaluable sourcebook for anyone who is interested in pursuing a course in these arts, and a perfect reference guide for those who are already involved.

KARATE

Karate is a self-defence system that utilizes the whole of the human body and the ways in which it moves and twists. Techniques vary from punching and striking with the fist, hands and elbows, to kicks and strikes with the feet, shins and knees. As with many of the martial arts, karate is often seen by those who have no experience of it as a "killing art", but to true practitioners the opposite is, in fact, the case. Karate, whether practised as an art, sport or as self-defence, carries the motto "never strike the first blow".

KARATE 空手

history *and* philosophy

Karate, or karate-do, loosely translated means "empty hand" (*kara* means "empty" and *te* means "hand"), and this art is indeed predominantly concerned with fighting with bare hands and feet. The basic principle is to turn the body into an effective weapon to defend and attack when and where it is appropriate.

Karate can be regarded as both a sport as well as a self-defence art depending on the emphasis of the club or association that is followed. Some instructors or coaches of karate place great emphasis on classical teachings, which incorporate traditional movements (such as *kata*) and philosophy, while others focus more on competition training. Some instructors, like Eugene Codrington, teach all aspects of the art. Karate is also an effective system of self-defence, which originally evolved on the Japanese island of Okinawa, where the carrying of weapons was forbidden, and so the inhabitants had to learn surreptitiously to protect themselves by other means.

Karate is one the most widely practised of the oriental martial arts. It evolved during one of the Japanese occupations of the island of Okinawa, part of the Ryukyu chain of islands, in the 15th century. Its roots, however, can be traced back much further than this – all the way back to ancient

A figure from the Shaolin Temple illustrates the connection between Okinawan karate, Japanese karate and weaponry.

India and China. Many people hold the view that what we today regard as the oriental martial arts have their roots in India. Indeed, when we look at such disciplines as yoga and the breathing techniques that originated in India, there does seem to be a great similarity between those and many of the modern martial arts systems.

It is believed that Zen Buddhist monks took the Indian fighting techniques to China from as early as the 5th and 6th centuries BC. Bodidharmi, the most famous of these monks, travelled at the end of the 5th century AD from India to China, where he became an instructor at the Shaolin monastery. He taught a combination of empty-hand fighting systems and yoga, and this became the well-known Shaolin kung fu – the system on which many Chinese martial arts systems are based.

In 1470, the Japanese had occupied the island of Okinawa. The law of the land dictated that anybody found carrying weapons would be put to death. In order to protect themselves from local bandits, who largely ignored the prohibition on weapons, Zen Buddhist monks developed the empty-hand system known as *te* ("hand"), importing new techniques from China. Eventually the new art was translated as *t'ang* ("China hand"), but was familiarly known as Okinawa-te ("Okinawa hand"). It was not until the 20th century that t'ang became known as karate-do ("empty hand"). The suffix *do* was added by Gichin Funakoshi's son Yoshitaka Funakoshi, in friendly opposition to his father's Okinawa-te style. Practice and demonstrations until that time had been extremely violent. Punches were not pulled and full contact was an integral part of the Okinawa-te style. Yoshitaka Funakoshi transformed the techniques of Okinawa-te into a gentler system, seeking not to deliver blows fully, but to "focus" strikes at skin level. The *do* suffix expressed the move away from the "aim of the warrior" and towards physical and spiritual development.

Gichin Funakoshi

Gichin Funakoshi (1868-1957) was a student of the Chinese classics and of the martial arts, and is credited with introducing karate to mainland Japan in the early part of the 20th century. Prior to this, in 1905, the occupying Japanese had authorized the inclusion of karate in the Okinawan physical education programme for middle school students. They appreciated the discipline inherent in karate and soon it became an integral part of the school educational system.

In 1917, at the request of the Japanese Ministry for Education, Funakoshi travelled from Okinawa to Kyoto in Japan and gave the first display of t'ang. In 1921, Funakoshi demonstrated his system for the Crown Prince of Japan at Shuri Castle. So impressive was this that Funakoshi was asked to appear at the first national athletic exhibition in Tokyo. Jiguro Kano, the founder of judo, among others, persuaded Funakoshi to stay on mainland Japan. In 1924, Funakoshi began teaching in several schools and *dojo* and founded the first University Karate Club at Keio University. Other styles started to develop, including kyokushinkai, shukukai and wado ryu. By 1936, karate had started to spread and the first purpose-built karate *dojo* was built, called shotokan (the "hall of shoto" – a pen name of

Funakoshi). The same year he published his second book, *Karate do Kyokan.*

In 1955 the first *dojo* of the Japan Karate Association was opened. Two years later in Tokyo, on 26 April, 1957, Funakoshi died. By this time, karate was well established, and today it is enjoyed throughout the world.

Styles

There are numerous styles of karate practised, and its influence even spreads into many other martial arts, so a book such as this cannot explore them all. This chapter will focus on the forms of wado ryu and shotokan. Hopefully, the information in this chapter will provide you with an insight into the world of karate, and allow you to decide if the discipline is for you.

It is also important to realize that the various styles of karate are the results of the personal ideas of many

Two senior karate sensei here illustrate attack and defence. Master Enoeda defends against Steve Arniel.

A senior student of Gichin Funakoshi – Hironori Ohtsuka – later devised his own "style" of karate: wado ryu.

Young children showing dedication to the art of karate.

individuals about how each basic technique should be carried out or applied. The different techniques within the styles of karate also dictate whether strength, speed, or hand or leg techniques are emphasized.

Karate as a sport

Karate has always been a self-defence system and a form of physical exercise. The competitive and sporting elements have a further part to play in the individual's enjoyment of this activity. It is because of the possibility of participation in competition that many people take up this art.

Competition comes in different forms, in which varying degrees of contact are allowed. In this book, we are concerned with traditional karate competition – sometimes termed sport karate. Certain dangerous techniques are omitted and strict rules are applied, making karate both safe and enjoyable for the competitor. One of the main purposes of karate competition is to show your skill at controlling the permitted techniques in a one-to-one combat situation. The individuals are allowed to move freely in a given area, which is controlled by a referee and a judge, or judges. *Kumite* is the word used to describe this type of competition.

Another form of competition that is also featured here is *kata*. *Kata* is a series of karate techniques performed alone against imaginary opponents. A *kata* competition resembles gymnastics or figure skating, in which points are awarded for correct technique and good balance, timing, rhythm, attitude and other attributes.

Competition is not the only reason for engaging in this art. It is possible to learn karate without participating in competitions – but for some people, competition provides stimulation and motivation for training. The sense of achievement that comes from just taking part, whether in *kata* or *kumite*, can be carried over into everyday life.

BENEFITS OF KARATE

The benefits derived from learning one of the forms of karate extend into many aspects of your everyday life. These include:

- Fitness, flexibility and mobility
- Well-being (through the balance of mind and body)
- Concentration and self-control
- Confidence
- Teamwork
- Honesty and integrity
- Stress reduction
- Sociability and courtesy

WADO RYU

history *and* philosophy

Hironori Ohtsuka (1892-1982) was the founder of the wado ryu system of karate. He commenced training in shindo yoshin ryu jujitsu at the age of six, and at the age of 30 he began training under the supervision of Gichin Funakoshi (the founder of karate-do) before founding the wado ryu system in 1939. Wado ryu is one of the four main Japanese styles of karate that are taught around the world. In 1939, Ohtsuka organized the All Japan Karate Do Federation Wado Ki and the Worldwide Headquarters for the Wado Ryu System. In 1967 he was the first *karateka* to be awarded the 5th order of merit of the sacred treasure of the Emperor of Japan as an acknowledgement of his achievements.

Following his death in 1982, Hironori Ohtsuka's son, Jiro, became the chief instructor of the wado ryu system. Today, there are a number of senior, well-respected representatives of wado ryu in Japan, who are also leaders of their own federations or associations.

Characteristics of wado ryu karate

To practitioners of wado ryu, the main philosophy is to better their attitude both within and outside the art. This is

Exhibition for the Crown Prince of Japan in 1921 at Shuri Castle.

Karate contains a number of airborne techniques.

The dove symbolizes a gentle or innocent person, as a means of advocating negotiation rather than violence.

one of the main aims of *budo* (martial art), which emphasizes the development of respect, discipline and understanding in a mental as well as physical capacity. This aim affects our attitude towards ourselves and others in our home life, work and social activities. To show aggression outwardly, even during training sessions, is greatly discouraged. The name wado ryu, approximately translated, means "the peaceful way".

Another characteristic of wado ryu is that unnecessarily large movements are kept to a minimum. Importance is placed on the speed and efficiency of movement with which each technique is performed, rather than the strength or physical effort outwardly shown. Exponents of wado ryu place great emphasis on the coordination of body movement with each particular technique. This principle is found in many other martial arts, such as ju-jitsu, aikido and kendo. This coordination is stressed at all stages of learning, from the execution of basic techniques to the application of advanced, free-fighting combinations.

Close quarter control is the underlying essence of karate.

BENEFITS OF WADO RYU

There are numerous benefits derived from learning wado ryu, which will extend into many aspects of everyday life. These include:

- Fitness
- Strength
- Confidence
- Self-discipline
- Self-control
- Sense of well-being
- Team work
- Concentration
- Integrity
- Sociability
- Courtesy

clothing *and* equipment

Karate practitioners wear a light, medium or heavy weight white cotton suit. The club badge or a combination is usually worn on the left side of the jacket. The white trousers have a drawstring waist and it is important to ensure you have the right size for comfort, practicality and safety. Protective equipment is used in karate by both men and women, especially in sparring (controlled fighting practice) and competition. Practitioners must be clean and tidy at all times, as a sign of respect to the art, teacher and fellow practitioner.

white belt

blue belt

white/yellow belt

purple belt

yellow belt

orange belt

brown belt

green belt

black belt

BELT GRADINGS

Beginners	White
10th-*kyu*	White
9th-*kyu*	White with yellow stripe
8th-*kyu*	Yellow
7th-*kyu*	Orange
6th-*kyu*	Green
5th-*kyu*	Blue
4th-*kyu*	Purple
3rd-*kyu*	Brown
2nd-*kyu*	Brown
1st-*kyu*	Brown
1st-*dan* and upwards	Black

PROTECTIVE EQUIPMENT

Extra protection in the form of groin protection (athletic cup) for men and breast protection for women are recommended for use at all times.

groin protection (athletic cup)

Bust protector

karate top

karate trousers

A smartly dressed karate instructor.

Etiquette

Training begins and ends with rituals of courtesy. These are an essential part of training and enable individuals to work safely and effectively together. Any distractions in a class could result in injury, and helping others to develop their abilities is an intrinsic part of being a good *karateka* (karate practitioner or student).

PRE-TRAINING DISCIPLINE

The instructor is always addressed by students as *sensei* (teacher or instructor). It is not quite accurate to translate *sensei* in this way, but for the sake of simplicity the word "teacher" will be used. It actually means "he who has gone before", indicating that whatever you are about to do or perform, your teacher will have done before, and understands its relevance.

There is nothing to distinguish one student (*karateka*) from another, other than the belt that is worn (*obi*), which is an acknowledgement of that person's experience. All *karateka* are equal as people, as indicated by a plain white cotton suit (*karate gi*). Juniors, seniors and masters alike must remove their footwear by the doorway and pause to bow (*rei*) before entering the training hall (*dojo*).

HELPFUL HINTS

- Training must be systematic, progressive and hard – technically as well as physically.
- Warm up before each training session and cool down afterwards.
- Constantly check and adjust the actions of individual techniques.
- Check the coordination of your movements for each technique.
- Practise all techniques using both sides of your body equally.
- Always be attentive to your opponent/partner (*zanshin*).
- If available, use a mirror to monitor your movements during training.
- If available, use punch bags or pads as aids for correcting specific actions.

❶ △ Stand upright and relaxed, hands in front of your thighs and with your fingers together and straight, thumbs tucked in. Place your heels together with your feet angled outwards, forming a V shape.

❷ △ Perform a bow (*rei*) by lowering the top part of your body by no more than 45 degrees. Keep your back straight and bend from the hips. Keep your eyes looking forwards. Bring your body back to the upright position.

❸ △ Turn slightly to the left and lower your body into a squatting position. Place your hands on top of your knees, which should naturally splay apart. Keep looking forwards while you maintain your balance.

❹ △ Complete the kneeling position by first placing your right knee, then your left knee, on the floor. Check that the distance between your knees is approximately one fist-width. Your feet must not be crossed while in this kneeling position and the tops of your insteps should be flat on the floor.

5 ◁ To perform the bow (*rei*) bring both hands around your knees and place them on the floor in front of your body. Your forefingers and thumbs should be touching in the shape of a V. Lower your upper body to perform the bow, stopping when your face is, depending on your size, about 10 in (25 cm) from the floor – it is not correct for your head to touch your hands. The object is to try to maintain a level body posture with your head and back in a straight line.

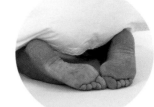

THE BOW

The bow is usually performed two or three times before practice begins. The order of the bows is fixed: the first bow is to *Shomen* (the Founder); the second is to the teacher (who is usually positioned towards the east); and the third bow is to each other.

◁ Seen from the rear, your big toes are touching and your insteps are flat to the floor.

6 △ Straighten your back and sit back in the kneeling position, in preparation to stand.

7 △ Start to return to the standing position by stepping forward with your left foot. Note the position of the rear right foot.

8 △ Once you are on your feet and standing in the original start position, perform a final bow.

MEDITATION

This position demonstrates the meditation (*mokuso*) position, which you use to clear your mind and prepare yourself for the practice to come. Keep your back straight and your shoulders relaxed.

There are two possible hand positions during meditation. The first is to place your hands in an open position on top of your knees. The more common hand position, however, is the one demonstrated here. Turn your palms upwards into a cupped position with the tips of the thumbs touching. Close your eyes and try to clear your mind of any concerns, worries or anxieties. Aim for a feeling of calmness and tranquillity. It is good to concentrate on your breathing to help empty your mind of any thoughts that could be a distraction. Keep your breathing slow, deep and controlled by inhaling through your nose and breathing out through your mouth.

In a normal practice session, hold this position for a minimum of 60 seconds. You may wish to build up this exercise so that you can hold the position for longer periods as part of your relaxation routine. If you are not used to sitting like this, build the exercise up gradually. Never hold a position if you feel pain. There is a certain amount of discomfort in stretching or learning new exercises, so always take your time.

Exercise | Warm-up

The following depict some of the exercises which are incorporated in the warm-up and cooling-down sessions. To reduce the risk of injuries, sound advice should be sought prior to starting any fitness or exercise programme. Usually the instruction will determine the length of time and number of repetitions each exercise requires. All the following are held for 3–10 seconds.

WARM-UP 1 – *This series of movements is a very gentle exercise designed to loosen up the neck and so minimize the risk of any injury during the practice session. It helps to stretch the muscles at the back of your neck as well as helping to relieve tension.*

①△ Stand in a relaxed position with your head upright.

②△ Carefully lower your chin downwards towards your chest. Keep relaxed and gently push down as if nodding to say "yes". Hold for 6–10 seconds and then return your head to the upright position.

③△ Continue the exercise with a side-neck stretch. Keep your head lowered and slowly move it towards your left shoulder.

④▷ Keeping your head facing forward, slowly lower your head towards the top of your left shoulder to stretch the muscles in the right side of the neck for 3–4 seconds. Repeat this exercise, lowering your head towards the right shoulder to stretch the left neck muscles.

⑤△ With the head in the upright position, turn your head so that you are looking over your right shoulder for 3 or 4 seconds. Repeat the exercise towards your left shoulder.

WARM-UP 2 – *The purpose of this series of exercises is to loosen and warm the body. This helps to avoid pulled muscles or torn ligaments during practice.*

❶ △ Keeping your arms bent from the elbows, rotate your arms in a full circular motion approximately 5–6 times, first clockwise, then anticlockwise (counterclockwise). This helps to stretch your shoulder muscles. Repeat 3–4 times in each direction.

❷ △ Stand in a relaxed position, feet apart. Push your left hand up and back five or six times. Reverse arm positions and repeat. This stretches your chest and shoulder muscles. Push back and release 2–4 times.

❸ △ Use a twisting motion to the right, bringing your arms in a circular action across your body and towards the rear. Repeat the exercise by turning towards the rear again. Hold for a few seconds then repeat the exercise to the left side.

❹ △ To stretch the sides of your body, stand in a relaxed position with your hands on your hips and feet apart. Lean slowly as far as possible to your right and extend your left arm as far as possible over your head. Hold for 3–10 seconds. Repeat the exercise to the opposite side by stretching your right arm towards your left side. Repeat this 2 or 3 times.

❺ △ Go into a squatting position and tuck your bottom in. Extend both arms forwards as far as possible at shoulder height. Hold this position for 3–10 seconds. This is excellent for stretching your lower back.

❻ △ With your legs fairly wide apart, slowly bend your right knee to lower your body towards that side. Hold at your lowest point for 3–10 seconds to stretch your inner thighs. Repeat this exercise to the other side and alternate 2 or 3 times.

❼ △ From an upright position, turn your body to the right. Come up on to the ball of your left foot and lower your body by bending your right knee. Hold the position at its lowest point for 3–10 seconds. Repeat to the left and alternate 2 or 3 times. This stretches your inner and upper thighs.

❽ ◁ From an upright position, move your right foot slightly in front of your left, keeping your back as flat as possible. Slowly lower your body, as if bowing from the waist, into a forwards position with your arms hanging forwards. Hold at your lowest point for 3–10 seconds, or longer if comfortable. Bend both knees before returning to the upright position. Repeat, starting with the left foot forward, and alternate 2 or 3 times.

❾ ▷ From a squatting position, move forwards on to your hands with your body raised – like a sprinter's start position in the blocks. Slowly press one heel down and backwards towards the floor. Hold for 3–10 seconds. Repeat the exercise with your other foot flat to the floor and alternate 4 or 5 times. This stretches your calf muscles.

Technique | *Kata – Pinan nidan*

The *kata – pinan nidan –* shown below is one of the first introduced to low grade students in most karate styles, with variation of technique depending on the particular style. *Kata* are a compilation of individual techniques put into various sequences, in which a practitioner encounters one or more imaginary opponent(s).

1 ◁ Take a few moments to focus your concentration on your imaginary opponent(s). Stand with your shoulders relaxed and make sure that your hands are open and lightly touching your thighs. *Note: a* kata *is designed to enable the practitioner to respond, defend and counter from a number of different angles and attackers. Emphasis is placed on good posture, coordination, timing and understanding basic technique and its application.*

2 ▷ Perform the bow (*rei*). Bow from the waist, but avoid bending too far forward. Keep your eyes alert and looking ahead.

◁ This is a side angle view of the bow.

3 ▷ To remain in a central position, and prepare for the natural standing position, *shizen-tai*, first move your left leg away from your right, followed by moving your right leg slightly away from your left leg. You should then be in a balanced position, with your feet shoulder-width apart, still splayed at approximately 20 degrees.

4 △ Move your left leg towards the left, dropping your body weight by bending your knees. At the same time take your left arm in a circular motion (as the arrow suggests) to your left side to perform the defence (*tetsui otoshi uke*). The bottom of the left fist is used to strike while the right fist is pulled back to your side. Keep your elbows tucked in.

5 △ Step through with your right leg, striking at the aggressor's solar plexus (*junzuki chudan*) with the right fist. For the next move, you will step to the rear, turning your body 180 degrees, following the direction of the arrows.

6 △ When you turn, perform a lower defence action (*gedan barai*) in a clockwise direction. This technique will stop a kick or punch aimed at your lower body.

7 △ Pull the right front leg backwards as you perform the hammer fist (*tetsui otoshi uke*) downward circular defence. The fist depicts a "hammer", hence the term, and can be used as both a defence and strike to an opponent.

8 ◁ Step through with your left leg and strike with your left fist to the opponent's solar plexus. Prepare to turn to the left, as the arrow shows, for the next move.

9 ▷ Turn and perform the lower sweeping defence (*gedan barai*). Keep your body upright, shoulders relaxed, and legs well braced. The key points of this stance are: feet a shoulder-width apart, back straight, eyes forward, back leg straight and a good bend on the front leg with your knee in line with your toes.

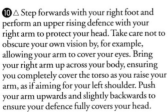

10 △ Step forwards with your right foot and perform an upper rising defence with your right arm to protect your head. Take care not to obscure your own vision by, for example, allowing your arm to cover your eyes. Bring your right arm up across your body, ensuring you completely cover the torso as you raise your arm, as if aiming for your left shoulder. Push your arm upwards and slightly backwards to ensure your defence fully covers your head.

11 △ Step through with your left foot and perform the same upper rising defence with your left arm. It is important to have a 45-degree bend on the forearm so that any attack is deflected, not met square-on. In this way, a blow making contact with the arm should slide downwards and away from you. If the forearm is horizontal, too much force will be directed on to one point and the result could be severe bruising, a fracture or a break.

12 ▷ Step through for a third time, performing the same upper rising defence with your right arm and using *kiai*. This is where you exhale with a short, sharp sound to emphasize your focus. The shout, or scream as it is sometimes called, can cause fear or distract your opponent. In the next move, your left leg will follow the direction of the arrow to the left, to initiate a turn.

13 △ Leading with your left leg, turn anticlockwise (counterclockwise) and utilize the lower sweeping defence.

14 △ Step through, right leg forward, and punch at your opponent's solar plexus with your right fist (*junzuki chudan*).

15 △ Move across to the right side, again performing the lower sweeping defence.

16 △ Step through with your left leg and punch with your left fist at your opponent's solar plexus (*junzuki chudan*).

17 △ Move 45 degrees in an anticlockwise (counterclockwise) direction and perform the lower sweeping defence.

18 △ Step through with your right leg and punch with your right fist to the solar plexus (*junzuki chudan*).

19 △ Step through again for a second *junzuki chudan* strike with your left leg and left fist forward.

20 △ Step through for a third time, with your right foot and right fist forward, and perform the *junzuki chudan* strike, this time using your shout (*kiai*).

21 △ Bring your left leg behind and across the rear of your body, turning in an anticlockwise (counterclockwise) direction into a cat stance, *neko ashi dachi*. About 70 per cent of your weight should be on your right leg. You are now in a position ready to defend and counter.

22 △ As you move through from one stance to another, try to maintain the same height i.e. do not push the body upwards or lower the body as you move forwards to each stance. By doing this, you make it more difficult for the aggressor to detect your intended movements.

23 △ Step through with your right leg, still maintaining the same body height, and keep your left arm extended.

24 ◁ Strike at your imaginary opponent with your open right hand, aiming at the lower abdomen (*yoko nukite*).

25 ▷ Take your right leg through 90 degrees into the cat stance (*neko ashi dachi*), with your right hand, palm uppermost, above the left, in preparation to strike. Reach forwards with your right leg in preparation for the next move.

26 ◁ Twist your body into a low stance (*shiko ashi dachi*) to perform the lower open-hand strike with your right hand. In the next move, you will step through with your left leg, in the direction of the arrow.

27 ◁ Step through with your left leg in preparation for the final strike.

28 ◁ Twist your body and strike, as previously, with your open left hand to the lower body (*yoko nukite*). In the next move, your left leg will move backwards in the direction of the arrow.

29 △ Now bring your left leg back to resume the upright standing position (*shizentai*).

30 △ Bring the left foot in, followed by the right, with the back of your heels together and feet splayed.

31 △ Bow again from the waist to complete the *kata* sequence. Maintain a calm and respectful manner, and keep alert until you have walked away from the practice area.

Technique | Two-person exercises – *Kumite*

Developing techniques in wado ryu is achieved through practising with a partner. The highest respect and discipline must always be maintained to preserve the values of the art and also to prevent injury. The following demonstrates the initial etiquette in preparation for the two-person practice (*kumite*) and some basic defence and striking actions.

1 △ Stand opposite your partner in the ready position approximately one metre's distance (minimum arm and a half distance).

2 △ Perform the etiquette bow (*rei*), keeping your eyes on your partner all the time.

3 △ Move into a stance known as the *hidari shizentai* position, ready to perform the techniques. In this position, the left foot is slightly forward in preparation to defend or attack.

4 △ You are grabbed at the front by your partner's left hand.

5 △ Perform a circular action with your left arm to enable the grip to be broken, stepping through with your left leg in preparation for the arm lock.

6 △ Once you have completed the circular movement, your opponent's grip will be broken and your partner will be in a vulnerable position.

7 ◁ Move through with your right leg and apply pressure to his left arm by maintaining the arm lock and strong upright posture.

8 ▷ Step through with your right leg and go into a deep (low) stance. Your partner's arm is now fully trapped by the application of pressure on his upper arm from your right elbow. From this position you can maintain the restraint or apply another technique that is applicable.

Technique | Blocking

Blocking is the term used to describe the defence method of arresting an attack, whether it be from an arm or leg strike. Various parts of the body, such as the forearm, palm heel and elbow, are used in a variety of ways to defend against an on-coming attack. This is complemented by the correct body movement for the nature of the attack.

❶ △ Step to the side and deflect your partner's kick by using a left lower forearm defence. The hand is made into a fist and a short circular action is used to deflect the kick. Note the right hand guard position.

❷ △ Pull your deflecting left arm around in a circular motion, bringing it down across your partner's neck and face. This action will push your partner backwards and off balance.

❸ ◁ A possible follow-on from this technique is to pull around behind your partner and apply a neck lock.

◁ Here you can see a more detailed side view of the previous neck lock.

Technique | Defence

There are a variety of very effective defensive moves in wado ryu which can be applied in a self-defence situation. The following is one such technique which demonstrates a combination of blocks and strikes, utilizing both hands and feet for different parts of the body.

❶ △ Your partner moves through with his right leg and right fist, aiming a punch at your face.

❷ ◁ Defend by stepping back and angling yourself slightly to the right. Use your left hand to deflect the blow downwards and, simultaneously, counter-strike with the palm of your right hand, aiming for the side of his jaw (mandible) – or deliver a front strike to his chin. Timing is important and the area to aim at depends on which is more accessible.

△ This angle of the action in step 2 shows how you deliver the palm blow.

❸ ▷ Pivot on your left leg and lift your right knee in preparation to strike with the top part of your foot to your partner's groin area.

△ In this close-up of step 3, you can see that the strike has been focused on the inner top part of the thigh. This is essential when practising to avoid injuring your partner. It is also advisable to wear groin protection when practising this type of technique.

Technique | *Taisabaki*

The following is a sample of three of the many *taisabaki* (evasive) techniques practised in wado ryu. The main principles behind these techniques consist of evasive manoeuvres to avoid contact if possible. *Taisabaki* practice increases the ability of the practitioner to move quickly in a variety of direction and be at an advantage to counter-strike.

1 ◁ As your partner moves in towards you with his left leg forward and right fist aimed towards your head, you should lean backwards to avoid contact.

2 ◁ As your partner steps through with *mai te zuki* (front punch delivered with the same arm and leg forward, or, right punch, right leg), drop and twist towards the right and take your left shoulder down towards the floor.

3 ▷ A defence against a *maigeri* (front kick) is achieved by twisting and side-stepping to avoid the kick.

SHOTOKAN

history *and* philosophy

Shotokan karate is both a young and an ancient martial art. It is ancient because its roots are deeply entrenched in the past, and young because, as it is expressed today, it is an art that is less than a hundred years old. Shotokan is characterized by its long, low stances, its powerful techniques and its dynamic forms.

The "founder" of shotokan, Gichin Funakoshi, was an Okinawan. He trained in the oldest of the Okinawan *te* ("hand") systems as a young man and in the early 20th century brought what he had learned in the island of Okinawa to mainland Japan, where he demonstrated his art before the Emperor. He originally intended to return to Okinawa but was persuaded to remain and continue teaching in Japan. Funakoshi's pen name was Shoto (which means "waving pines"), and *kan* means "hall", so shotokan karate can be translated to mean, "Shoto's hall of the way of the empty hand".

While Funakoshi was the orignator of shotokan, it was really his son, Yoshitaka Funakoshi, who developed it into the form we know today. It rapidly grew in popularity, supported, encouraged and regulated by the powerful Japan Karate Association, and before long was to be found all over the world.

Shotokan has produced some of the world's greatest karate exponents, including Hirokazu Kanazawa. It is believed by many *karateka* (karate practitioners) that

Hirokazu has come closest to possessing the most perfect technique. He studied karate at Takushoku University and won all the Japan Championships in 1962, with a broken hand after his mother had persuaded him to fight. Shotokan continues to be practised by thousands of people, adults and children, throughout the world.

Triads

Shotokan karate is built on what are known as "triads", which are both real organizations and metaphors for some-

Early days of shotokan karate in a dojo *in Tokyo. Notice the traditional* tatami *mat flooring.*

thing much deeper within the human psyche. There exists the physical triad of *kihon* (basics), *kumite* (sparring) and *kata* (forms), which require dedicated training and the constant perfecting of technique. This is followed by the moral triad of justice, mercy and compassion and finally by the ethical triad of duty, honour and loyalty.

If you put all of the nine triad principles together (nine symbolizes perfection) you achieve the whole, rounded person. When these principles are practised in a martial art, they illustrate one of the fundamental concepts of shotokan karate, as advocated by the founder, Gichin Funakoshi. His aim was to focus on the development of the human character as a whole being, rather than on winning and losing.

Quite apart from the normal reasons why somebody would take up a martial art, such as self-defence, there are other reasons that, while they may not be clear at the time, emerge during the course of training. Shotokan not only provides the means to defend yourself against an aggressor, it also gives you a sense of self-confidence. Self-confidence stimulates a sense of well-being and a greater sense of awareness when in difficult situations. It also heightens your consciousness of the environment and the very nature of unjust aggression. In this context, the *karateka* (students of karate) can make a mature and reasoned judgement as to what response, if any, to make – provided, of course, that the response conforms to the rules laid down by law, governing the use of reasonable force.

In this sense, shotokan (and the pursuit of excellence) brings with it grave responsibilities that must be exercised with compassion and mercy. The physical development and improvement of technique and ability is useless without this other dimension. Ultimately, karate exists to perfect the individual, to produce men and women who are just,

Taiji Kase, a senior member of the shotokan fraternity, illustrates the Chinese influence upon modern-day karate.

compassionate and honourable members of society, people who recognize injustice and, through their own behaviour, challenge it.

While shotokan is a wonderful form of relaxation or sport for many people, for those who practise it seriously it has a much wider and deeper significance. But this deeper realization can come only after years of dedicated practice. While this is a dimension of the art that emerges only slowly, karate can still be enjoyed at all levels by hundreds of thousands of people throughout the world.

Harada Sensei, a direct student of Gichin Funakoshi, defends against a double-wrist grab.

BENEFITS OF SHOTOKAN

The benefits derived from learning shotokan extend into many aspects of your everyday life. These include:

• Fitness, flexibility and mobility
• Well-being (through the balance of mind and body)
• Concentration and self-control
• Confidence and assertiveness
• Teamwork
• Honesty, integrity and humility
• Appreciation of justice and fair play
• Stress reduction
• Sociability and courtesy

clothing *and* equipment

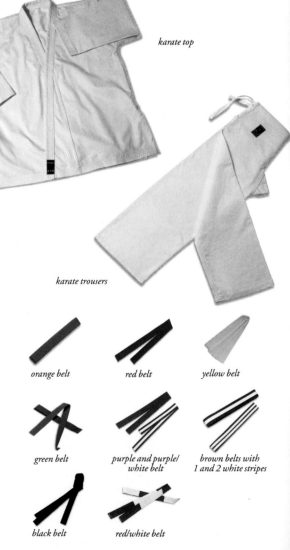

Shotokan practitioners wear a white cotton top and drawstring trousers. Most schools follow the belt grading system below, with beginners usually wearing a white or blue belt.

At 3rd-*dan* a *karateka* may be addressed as "*sensei*". At 4th-*dan* it is assumed that the *karateka* is well acquainted with the style and has a deep knowledge of the technical syllabus. A 5th-*dan* can be awarded after the writing of a technical thesis on karate. All *dan* grade awards after this are for progress within shotokan, with emphasis on style, devotion, dedication and commitment to the art. With the award of 6th-*dan* can come the title "*shihan*" which freely translated means "master" or literally "a teacher of teachers". At this stage the *karateka* is regarded as a master of his/her style and is given the right to wear the red and white belt or may continue to wear the black belt. Although it may take 30 years of hard, disciplined training and study to achieve 6th-*dan*, this may only be the beginning of the pursuit of excellence.

karate top

karate trousers

BELT GRADINGS

9th-*kyu*	Orange
8th-*kyu*	Red
7th-*kyu*	Yellow
6th-*kyu*	Green
5th-*kyu*	Purple
4th-*kyu*	Purple with white stripe
3rd-*kyu*	Brown
2nd-*kyu*	Brown with one white stripe
1st-*kyu*	Brown with two white stripes
1st–5th-*dan*	Black
5th-*dan* upwards	Black or red and white

orange belt

red belt

yellow belt

green belt

purple and purple/white belt

brown belts with 1 and 2 white stripes

black belt

red/white belt

Etiquette

In shotokan karate there are three types of bow (*rei*) used in different circumstances – namely: *shomen ni rei*, performed as a sign of respect to the training area; *otagani rei*, performed to the great masters of the past and present; and *shihan rei*, which is used by both teachers and students.

OTAGANI REI – *Bow performed to the great masters of the past and present.*

❶ △ Stand in a natural position (*hachichi dachi*), with your feet splayed slightly outwards and with your hands hanging relaxed at the sides of your body. Keep looking forwards.

❷ △ Move your right leg in towards your left so that your heels are touching.

❸ △ Turn your left shoulder forwards.

❹ △ Lower your body towards the floor, placing your left knee on the floor and make sure that you keep looking forwards.

❺ △ Place your right knee on the floor, aligning it with your left, and place your hands on top of your thighs.

❻ △ Leaning slightly forwards from the kneeling position (*seiza*), place your left hand in front of your body.

❼ △ Follow through with your right hand so that your forefingers and thumbs make a triangular shape. Make sure that you keep looking forwards.

❽ △ Bend forwards from the waist, keeping your fingers in the same position and your gaze forwards. Reverse the process back into kneeling and stand.

Exercise | Warm-up

In shotokan karate, the warm-up exercises are very similar to those in wado ryu karate, covered in the first section of this chapter. Those below are just a sample of the exercises performed prior to a training session. Make sure that you approach every exercise gently and with caution. Build up at your own pace to an acceptable and comfortable level.

WARM-UP 1 – *This exercise is designed to stretch your triceps, back and chest area.*

◁ Bring your left arm across the back of your head and place your right hand on your left elbow. Pull your elbow in a downwards motion towards your right side. Repeat 2 to 3 times each side.

▷This is a rear view of the position when the exercise is performed on the other side. It shows the correct arm and hand positions, with your right hand on the left shoulder blade and your left hand gripping your right elbow.

WARM-UP 2 – *The following movement exercises the fingers and assists in making the wrists more supple.*

❶ △ Push your hand downwards and outwards, keeping your fingers open and splayed.

❷ △ Push your fingers well back, with your palm facing upwards, using a downwards rocking motion. Hold this position for several seconds and perform the same exercise on the opposite side. Repeat the whole exercise once more.

WARM-UP 3 – *This exercise is beneficial for your back, hips and thighs promoting suppleness and flexibility.*

▷ Sit on the floor and cross your right leg over your left, keeping your right knee bent. Look to the rear so that you stretch the upper part of your body as well as the lower back, hip and upper thighs. Make sure that your right hand is placed well behind you so that you feel securely balanced. Place your left arm across the outside of your right knee and twist your body backwards. Hold this position for approximately 20 seconds, then reverse leg and hand positions and repeat 2 or 3 times each side.

WARM-UP 4 – *This exercise stretches your inner thighs and leg muscles and promotes good body balance.*

WARM-UP 5 – *This exercise will stretch the back of your thighs and calf muscles.*

△ Place your right leg to the side to adopt a wide stance. Then carefully lower your body so that your left knee is well bent and your right leg is straight, toes facing forwards. Keep your hands stretched out in front of you, palms facing forwards, and your right hand gripping your left. If you have not performed this, or a similar exercise before, it may take a lot of practice to maintain your balance while stretching. Hold this position for approximately 20 seconds, then reverse leg positions and repeat 2 or 3 times for each side.

△ Place your left foot in front of your right, with your heel down and toes facing up. Place both hands on your left thigh, pushing your hips back and leaning forwards with the top part of your body. Hold for several seconds and reverse the leg position. Repeat 2 to 3 times.

Technique | Basics

Learning a series of basic techniques has always been very important to all martial art traditions. In this way, you build a good foundation on which all moves can be correctly and safely executed. Some of these moves will be common to two or more different martial arts, while others may be unique.

ZENKUTSU DACHI – Shotokan, in particular, is well known for its use of a very low stance called zenkutsu dachi, *or front stance. This is used in the majority of the basic moves.*

JUDACHI – This stance is a shorter version of the front stance and is more suitable for close-quarter combat, competition and basic self-defence moves.

◁ Note that your legs should not be positioned as low as in the classic front stance. Keep both hands in a protective position in front of your body. Practise this stance, moving forwards and backwards with both your right and left legs.

△ From the natural position, with your feet shoulder-width apart, step forwards into a low stance with your left leg. Keep your back leg straight with the heel flat on the floor. Make sure the knee of your leading leg is bent to an angle of approximately 90 degrees.

KOKUTSU DACHI – An effective defensive move.

KIBA DACHI – This position is known as the horse stance.

△ Step forwards with your left leg, distributing your body weight so that about 70 per cent is on the rear leg. Hold your hands in a protective open hand (fingers straight) position, with the right hand covering the solar plexus and the left hand in the guard position ready to defend or strike. Practise on both sides.

△ Move your right leg to the side into a low posture similar to that of riding a horse. The knees must be bent well forwards, with heels parallel to each other and feet facing forwards. Keep your back straight and your hands in a closed hand (fist) guard position. Practise this stance, moving forwards and backwards alternating between your left and right leg.

Neko Ashi Dachi – The feeling of feline lightness and poise gives this position its name of "cat stance".

◁ Move forwards with your left leg, ensuring that about 90 per cent of your weight is on the back leg. Practise this stance, moving forwards and backwards with both your right and left legs. Ensure that your knees are well bent and your right hand is placed on your right hip ready to execute a technique, while your left hand is in the lower guard position.

Sanshin Dachi – The hand and foot positions give the figure a pinched-looking middle, accounting for its name of "hour-glass stance".

◁ With your feet about a shoulder-width apart and your right foot slightly in front, turn your feet inwards and slightly bend your knees. Keep your back upright, chin straight and eyes looking forwards. The hands are in the ready position to strike, with the left hand at shoulder level and right hand on the waist. Use the palm heel to strike both the face and groin simultaneously. Repeat on the other side.

Fuda Dachi (Sochin) – Because of the very low, strong body position, this is known as "the rooted stance".

▷ Move forwards with your leading leg, ensuring that about 90 per cent of your weight is on the back leg. Practise this stance, moving forwards and backwards with both your right and left legs. This low posture is excellent for developing strong calves and thigh muscles. The clenched fists are positioned to protect the face and body prior to striking, if necessary.

GUARD POSITION

It is very important to protect your body when being confronted and/or practising. The stance you adopt will dictate the most appropriate hand guard position. This can vary from having both hands in front of the torso, with one hand just above the other, to having one hand in front of the face (but not obscuring vision) and the other in the lower body region. This strategic position ensures the body is effectively covered and ready either to defend or to strike.

Technique | Defence and blocking

Shotokan embodies a variety of defence and blocking techniques. *Kata* (set forms where the practitioner defends and strikes an imaginary opponent) also differ in application and shotokan has, in addition, its own unique *kata*. The following are a sample of two of the basic blocking techniques used. They can be practised in isolation or with a partner.

Soto uke (**body block**) – *This is a defensive move against an attack to the chest (middle body) area.*

❶ ◁ Stand with feet together and bring your right arm in line with the back of your head. Simultaneously bring your left arm in front of your upper chest. As you start to move forwards with your right leg, into a low stance, bring your right fist through in a circular motion. At the same time, pull your left hand back on to your left hip.
Note: Imagine you have a piece of string attached to both hands, and as the left hand pulls back, so it brings the right arm into position.

❷ ◁ Keep looking towards your opponent and maintain a strong posture as you deliver this technique. Keep your left fist well back on your left hip and right arm in a bowed position. Aim to use the inside of your forearm, near the elbow, when delivering the block against the opponent's strike.

Gedan barai (**lower body block**)

◁ From the natural position (*hachichi dachi*), make a fist with both hands and bring your left fist across your chest, in line with your right collar bone. Step forwards with your left foot into *zenkutsu dachi* stance. At the same time, bring the left arm across your body in a downwards motion to finish with the left fist approximately 4–5 inches (10–13 cm) above the left knee. This blocking action is very effective against lower body strikes, especially kicking techniques.

Technique | Kicking

Shotokan embodies a selection of strong kicking techniques to the front, side and rear of the body. Kicking techniques have two applications. The first is *keage* (shown here), which means to strike in a "snapping action", such as kicking with a fast retraction. The second variation is *kekome*, which emphasises thrusting and using the heel.

1 △ Move into the low horse stance (*kiba dachi*). Make sure that your hands are in the guard position.

2 △ Bring your left leg across your right, making sure that the knees are locked in a "scissor" position.

3 ▷ With your guard still in position, bring your right leg up to the side of your body and push outwards, striking towards one of your imaginary opponent's vulnerable areas, such as the face, solar plexus, floating rib or groin. This is known as *yoko geri*. Make sure that you twist your foot to the side so that the "knife edge" of the foot will be tense – this is the part that delivers the technique. To assist in this action, push your toes inwards and downwards while keeping your foot horizontal.

4 ◁ Bring your kicking foot back in a snapping action, in line with your left knee. It is important to bring your foot back before going down into a fighting posture, to avoid having your leg swept away from under you. It also allows you the freedom to choose where you wish to position your stance: forwards, side or back.

5 ▷ Go back down into the *kiba dachi* posture, still in fighting stance, keeping your eyes on your opponent.

Technique | *Soto uke* block

It is very important to practise basic techniques, such as this blocking/counter-attacking exercise, working from both right and left positions. If you are right-handed and have a weak left hand/foot, work twice as hard with the left side so that you can balance the strength of your skill. This applies to all techniques.

1 △ Bow to show respect to your partner. Remember the "respect but no trust" principle, which is why it is important to look at your opponent, not down towards the floor.

2 △ Your partner steps back with his right foot, preparing to strike your solar plexus region. Note the low front posture (*zenkutsu dachi*).

3 ◁ You step back with your right leg into the formal *zenkutsu dachi* stance and defend with the middle body block (*chudan soto uke*). This is a block from outside inwards. Apply this defence by starting with your left fist in line with your left ear and, using a circular motion, bring your arm forwards, around and across your body. Make sure you turn your forearm inwards so that it is the muscle part of the arm that makes contact with the incoming blow. At the same time, pull your left shoulder back so that your body turns to the side, thus becoming a smaller target.

4 ◁ Whether you block with your left or right arm dictates where you punch your opponent. In this case, when you have executed your block, use a downwards motion to push the attacking arm away. A circular action draws the opponent or partner off-centre and exposes his chest area in preparation for your counter-attack, a front-lunge punch (*oi-tsuki*).

5 ▽ Deliver a strike to your opponent's solar plexus region with your right fist. Remember to maintain a low, strong posture (*zenkutsu dachi*).

Technique | Elbow strike and wrist take-down

The following demonstrates a sequence of moves utilizing *soto uke* block, elbow strike (*empi*) and wrist locks (*kokuto*) to restrain the opponent. There are various sequences in shotokan where the basics are applied and developed incorporating more advanced techniques. It is important to utilize your strengths against the opponent's weaknesses.

❶◁ Step back and perform *soto uke* block to the right fist attack from your opponent.

❷▷Immediately follow through with an elbow *empi* strike to the hinge of your opponent's jaw.

❸▷ Bring your right hand back to your opponent's right wrist in preparation to apply a wrist turn and lock.

△ This close-up shows in detail the position of your hands and fingers on your opponent's hand.

4 ▽ Start to rotate your opponent's wrist by turning the hand outwards so that the palm is facing upwards. Next, ensure your thumbs are secure on the back of his hand, with your fingers firmly wrapped around his lower hand and wrist.

◁ This close-up shows in more detail the position of your hands and fingers on your opponent's hand.

5 △ Maintain the lock and keep the momentum going as you start to push the hand downwards, forcing your opponent to submit.

6 ▽ Continue to push downwards so that your partner will be restrained on the floor.

7 ▷ As your opponent reaches the floor, bring your left leg forwards and over his right arm. Aim to turn your body 180 degrees and apply pressure on his elbow joint as your body moves over his right arm.

8 ▷ The follow-on advanced technique is an arm lock. Bring your right leg over and across your opponent's arm and turn around so that you are facing in the opposite direction. Slowly lower your body so as to apply pressure on his elbow joint and form an arm lock. When practising with a partner always take care to apply this technique slowly and with caution.
Note: This is an advanced technique which requires qualified supervision.

AIKIDO

合気道

Aikido is an art that teaches one to harmonize completely with any attack, leading an aggressor to a point of imbalance, and then applying a neutralizing technique. Some practitioners believe that it is possible to study aikido as a spiritual discipline alone, whereby students learn to unite their spiritual energy with the universe to become "one with nature". It is equally possible to study aikido as a dynamic system of combat. For most individuals, however, the reality of aikido training falls between these two positions.

AIKIDO

history *and*
philosophy

Aikido in its present form is a relatively recent innovation within the martial arts tradition, and was developed in Japan in the early 20th century by Morihei Ueshiba (1883-1969), who was introduced to the classical martial arts as a boy by his father, Yoroku. He is known to have studied some martial arts, such as various styles of ju-jitsu as well as kenjutsu and the art of the spear. In 1912 Morihei moved to Hokkaido, where a chance meeting with a man called Sokaku Takeda changed his life.

Takeda was a master of daito ryu-aiki ju-jutsu, a martial art that had originated in the 6th century AD and had been passed down through the military hierarchy and formalized by members of the Aizu clan, becoming known as the Oshikiuchi, or "striking arts". The young Ueshiba quickly became drawn to the fierce demeanour of this little man, and studied under Takeda until 1919. On returning to his native Tanabe on the death of his father, Morihei met Onisaburo Deguchi – the charismatic founder of an esoteric religion called Omoto-Kyo – and spent the next six years as his disciple, travelling throughout Asia.

In 1927, Morihei set up the Kobukan *dojo* in Tokyo and began teaching an amalgam of the martial traditions he had learned from Takeda, together with the spiritual beliefs he had gleaned from Deguchi. This new discipline he called Ueshiba aiko-budo. Morihei finally settled on the name of aikido. This word is a combination of three concepts: *ai*

meaning "harmony"; *ki* meaning "spirit"; and *do* meaning "way". In the spiritual sense, this means harmonizing your individual spirit, or *ki*, with the spirit of Nature itself. In the *dojo*, this means that you harmonize with an attack, lead it to a point of exhaustion and then neutralize it with a throw, joint lock, or an immobilization.

As with many other martial arts, aikido is seen not only as a system of self-defence, but also as a means of self-cultivation and improvement. Today there are various systems of aikido, but traditional aikido has no tournaments, competitions or contests. Physical strength is not a prerequisite, so age is no impediment. According to Morihei Ueshiba, the goal of aikido is not the defeat of others, but the defeat of the negative characteristics that inhabit one's own mind and inhibit its effective functioning.

What is aikido?

If you look at the classic Chinese *yin* and *yang* icon, you see a symbol explaining that all phenomena are governed by antagonistic, yet complementary opposites, forming the two halves of the whole. You will also observe that the two halves are not entirely opposite, however, since they have elements of each other within them – the black dot in the white half and white dot in the black half – and this esoteric symbolism is designed to suggest that all of life and nature is in a perpetual state of flux.

The antagonistic yet complementary opposites of the Chinese yin *and* yang *icon underly the philosophy behind aikido.*

If you are attacked by a force (*yang*) and you apply force yourself (*yang*), a collision of energies ensues which results in disharmony, and accordingly the strongest force wins. If, however, you meet that force with an absorbing movement (*yin*) and then exhaust it to the point of imbalance before applying a force of your own (the aikido way), you are, in effect, restoring harmony or redressing an imbalance. This is the basic logic and underlying philosophy of aikido.

Aikido is a discipline that seeks not to meet violence with violence, but instead looks towards harmonizing with and restraining an opponent. Aikido is, in many ways, unique among the martial arts, in that the majority of techniques are based on the aggressor making the first move. Therefore, aikido techniques are usually aimed at joint immobilization, and throws which utilize an opponent's energy, momentum and aggression. Many body movements have been taken from Japanese sword and spear fighting arts, and the use of the *bokken*, (a replica sword), and *jo* (a stick), is intended to develop the practitioner's understanding and skill.

Aikido teaches one-on-one and multiple-attack defence. It incorporates knife-taking, sword- and stick-taking, and even defence from a kneeling position. Differences in size, weight, strength or age are negated, as you learn to use your inner *ki* (flow of energy). Weapon training with a *bokken* and *jo* indicates the ancestry of the discipline as well as helping to improve your body movements. Most of these techniques are covered in this book.

It should be emphasized that aikido is a *budo* – literally a "martial way". You practise each technique with total commitment, as if your life depended on its success, for only in this way is it possible to bring about the true spirit of *budo*. This is not to say that training has to be hard or violent: it is possible to be physically soft and still generate the power to control a confrontational encounter.

Training

By training cooperatively with a partner, you can practise even potentially lethal techniques without risk, but professional supervision and safe practice are always required for students to avoid injury. Mutual respect and the careful consideration of what you are learning, together with its consequences, must always be your main concern. There are no shortcuts or easy paths to ability in aikido. Attaining proficiency is simply a matter of sustained and dedicated training, just as it is in many of the martial arts disciplines. Nobody becomes an expert in a few months.

While there are different styles of aikido – such as tomiki, or sport aikido, in which rubber knives are used and practitioners compete to score points – the founder, Morihei Ueshiba, was firmly opposed to competition in any form.

Styles of aikido

In reality, there are several major styles of aikido today. As Ueshiba was continually refining and modifying the art he had created, some of his students at various stages left to pursue their own ideals. Thus, Master Gozo Shioda created the yoshinkan style, characterized by short, sharp movements and powerful joint applications; Kenji Tomiki created sport aikido, as it is widely known, characterized by competitions in which rubber knives are used; Minoru Mochizuki successfully amalgamated aikido with other martial arts within the International Martial Arts Federation; and Koichi Tohei created shin-shin toitsu aikido, which concentrates on the *ki* aspect of aikido. All of these men trained with and listened to Ueshiba and yet each came away with a different idea of the discipline.

The grading system

The grading in aikido consists of *kyu* (student) grades, 6th to 1st, after which students become eligible for a 1st-*dan* (1st-

Demonstrating one of aikido's flowing movements and flexibility of practitioners.

Demonstrating the dynamics of aikido in action, showing gyaku *(reverse)* kotegaeshi *(outward wrist twist).*

degree black belt), and then 2nd-*dan*, 3rd-*dan* and so on. These gradings are based on a National grading syllabus and are spaced apart according to the dictate of the clubs' governing association.

There are no coloured belts in traditional aikido, except for children. This is in accordance with directives from the *hombu* (headquarters) in Japan. Because there are no weight or strength divisions, it is possible for men, women and children to train together, although certain techniques are eliminated from children's practice for safety reasons.

As a first step, students learn how to fall properly and how to absorb the effects of the various techniques, so that they can be performed with total commitment. Next is the freestanding solo body movements, where students learn about shifting weight, balance and similar aspects of the discipline. Finally, the techniques themselves are taught, and the degree of difficulty is dependent on each individual's own progress.

Benefits of aikido

People learn aikido for a variety of reasons: as a way of becoming physically fit, as self-defence, or to understand something of Japanese culture. It is up to each individual to decide upon which facet of the discipline to concentrate. In addition to the development of strength, stamina and suppleness, students learn to tap their internal powers to generate an energy that is far greater than muscular power alone, and to use it at will. Students may also find mental stimulation in knowing that they are practising movements dating back to Japan's feudal past.

Breathing techniques are learned to promote mind and body coordination. Students also come into contact with other Japanese practices, such as shiatsu (finger therapy), a form of total body massage, and iaido (Japanese sword drawing). Both of these disciplines are complementary to the study of aikido and are occasionally taught in tandem.

BENEFITS OF AIKIDO

Aikido offers many benefits to enhance health and well-being including:

- Enhances strength, stamina and suppleness
- Promotes a good mental attitude and discipline
- Promotes defensive moves as opposed to aggression
- Increases your awareness of danger
- Increases body reflexes
- Promotes a calmness of mind
- Develops internal energy and power

clothing *and* equipment

In accordance with directives from *hombu* (headquarters) in Japan, adult students do not wear coloured belts, although the *kyu* (student) grading system still applies.

It is acceptable for children to wear coloured belts and the student system starts at 6th-*kyu*, which requires the wearing of a white belt with one red stripe. Children then progress through a number of coloured stripes and belts until they reach 1st-*kyu*, which is the final *kyu* grade before they are ready to take their black belt (1st-*dan*).

When students pass the examination for their 1st-*dan* (*shodan*), they are entitled to wear a *hakama* (a divided/pleated skirt). This is considered an honour and the grade is recorded at hombu. Students also receive a membership card, an international *yudansha* (*dan*-grade) record book and a certificate signed by the founder's son, Doshu (Kisshomaru Ueshiba).

Students who set an example or who work exceptionally hard for the benefit of the club i.e. administration, may be awarded permission to wear a hakama before they attain dan grade, subject to the senior instructor's discretion.

Smartly dressed with hakama tied correctly, prior to commencement of training.

black hakama

While practising aikido you will study the use of the bokken *(wooden sword), knife techniques and* jo *(a stick). This study is complementary to that of aikido. The* jo *should reach from the ground to just under the arm/shoulder, and it should be smooth and free from splinters for both safety and to allow free-flowing movements. The* bokken *or* bokuto *is a wooden sword made from Japanese oak (red or white), approximately the same size and shape as the sword (* katana*).*

jo

bokken *or* bokuto

Etiquette

Aikido has strict codes of discipline and etiquette. These are necessary to ensure that the original spirit and attitude towards the art are maintained, with respect for the *dojo* and each other being observed at all times. A casual attitude towards training could result in injury. Care and courtesy should always be maintained.

RESPECTING THE FOUNDER – *In most traditional aikido dojos, it is very important to have a picture of the founder, Morihei Ueshiba. This may be positioned on the dojo floor, or on a table or wall, but it should be positioned centrally at the front of the dojo, or kamiza (meaning "seat of the Gods").*

❶ △ Sit facing the picture of Morihei Ueshiba in a kneeling position (*seiza*). Make sure that your back is straight, feet are together and you are sitting on your heels. Your knees need to be about two fist-widths apart and, ideally, with the big toe of your right foot over the big toe of your left. Push your shoulders back and stay relaxed.

❷ △ Place your left hand in front of your body, with your fingers pushed together and your thumb forward, so that when the right hand meets the left they form a triangle.

❸ △ Bow deeply towards the *kamiza* . Make sure that your back is straight, and do not let your head touch the floor.

BOWING TO A PARTNER – *Demonstrating respect prior to practising with a partner.*

❶ △ When practising with a partner, the same form is followed. Sit opposite your partner, ensuring that there is a reasonable distance between you (usually an arm and a half). The bow (*rei*) is performed again, to show respect towards your partner. This seated bow is called *zarei*.

❷ △ Using the same hand and body positions as those in the bow (*rei*) to the *kamiza*, perform the bow towards your partner. Both partners bow simultaneously to show mutual respect.

THE BOW

Why, when and how to bow are natural questions raised by anyone taking up aikido. Most practitioners find that they soon adopt the custom and very quickly come to understand and enjoy the ritualized etiquette as an important part of their training process.

Correct etiquette is, above all, an expression of respect and courtesy to those with whom you are training. On entering the *dojo* (training room), perform a standing *rei* (bow) to the *kamiza* (desig-

nated area of respect where the instructor sits). Once you have asked, and been given permission to enter on to the mat (*tatami*) by the highest grade holder, perform a further standing *rei*. Practitioners then line up in a kneeling position, facing the *kamiza* in grade order: *kohei* (beginners) to the left of *sempai* (seniors), with the most senior on the right side of the *dojo*. You then wait until the class instructor comes on to the mat.

Exercise | Warm-up

Aikido, as with other martial arts, uses certain exercises to prepare the body for training and to ensure that muscles and tendons are warmed and stretched to avoid injury during practice. The exercises are designed to simultaneously stretch many areas of the body. Below are a selection that relate specifically to aikido.

WARM-UP 1 – *This exercise is performed on the legs, arms and torso, and is used to make the body more supple and relaxed. This is achieved through the gentle tapping action against the skin, which relaxes muscles and encourages blood to come to the surface of the skin.*

WARM-UP 2 – *After relaxing the body as in warm-up 1, you are ready to engage in stretching exercises. The following exercises continue to enhance blood circulation, while stretching the upper body.*

△ Place your right arm across your upper chest area and your left hand on your right elbow. Push your right arm as far around your body as you comfortably can, and half close your right fist. Starting at the back of the neck area, tap your body, working your way across the shoulder and down the arm.

△ With feet astride, drop the top half of your body forwards and swing your arms to either side. Keep your arms straight and look towards the arm that is moving in an upwards direction. This ensures that you fully stretch your body, in particular the waist, hips and arms.

◁ With your feet shoulder-width apart, lower your body, spreading your feet so that they face outwards. Place your elbows inside your knees with hands open and palms facing outwards. Gently push outwards to stretch your inner thighs. Repeat several times, trying to push a little further each time.

WARM-UP 4 – *Yoga type stretch and* tanden *(centre of gravity) exercise.*

❶ ◁ With your legs astride, as far apart as you can comfortably manage, lower your body, elbows together and fists clenched, cushioning your forehead. It is very important to ensure that you have your elbows together, since this helps to stretch your upper body.

❷ △ Push your hands forwards and open them in preparation to bringing them around in a circular motion.

❸ △ As you push your hands forwards, have a feeling of using your stomach area (centre of gravity). It is a feeling of pushing your energy in a projected, forward motion. Bring your hands back into the centre position. Repeat this entire sequence 3 to 4 times.

Exercise | Loosening the neck

This exercise helps to loosen the muscles and tension in the back of the neck. The everyday stresses of life can cause tension and tightening in the back of the neck. Such tension can be relieved through the regular application of appropriate exercises. The following demonstrates one of the basic methods to enhance blood flow and stimulate muscles and tendons in the back of the neck.

◁ Place your right hand at the back of your neck, palm downwards and fingers pushed together. With the knife edge side of your hand, use a gentle "chopping" action, then gradually work up from the lower neck to the base of the skull, and then back down to the base. Repeat this exercise with your left hand on the opposite side of your neck.

Exercise | Kneeling practice

Kneeling techniques (*suwariwaza*) date back to the days of the *samurai*. Most aikido techniques can be practised from this position. Their primary purpose is to teach economy of movement and to make you aware of your *tanden* (centre) and hips. The techniques also promote flexibility in the lower limbs.

❶ △ Go down into a kneeling position with your left knee raised and your right knee lowered towards the floor. You should be on the balls of your feet with your heels close together. Keep your body upright with your hands forward as a defensive guard. Make sure you are looking forwards, not at the floor or around the *dojo*.

❷ △ Move forwards by placing the left knee down on to the floor and swivelling on it as you bring your right knee forwards. Swivel your knee and hips together to move forwards. This exercise is useful as a means of helping to develop the lower part of your body and is known as "walking on your knees" (*shikko*).

Exercise | Wrist flexibility

Many of the aikido techniques apply strong pressure to the wrist, elbow and shoulder joints. With great emphasis on fluent and supple movement, wrist exercises play an important part in the warm-up procedures. The exercises follow a prescribed technique, with each movement preparing the practitioner for the relevant method.

EXERCISE 1 – *The purpose of this exercise, known as* kote gaeshi *("wrist-out turn"), is to enhance the flexibility of your hands and wrists.*

△ Take hold of your left hand with your right hand. Push downwards and inwards in a twisting motion, pulling inwards towards your sternum. Ensure that your elbows are at about 90 degrees to your body and are horizontal. Repeat this exercise 2 or 3 times each side.

EXERCISE 3 – *This exercise is used in preparation for the technique called* shiho nage *or four-direction throw.*

❶ ◁ Take hold of your left hand at the centre of your body, with the palm of your right hand on top of the back of your left, fingers facing upwards. Keep your hands close to your chest and ensure that your elbows are down and arms tucked in close to your body. The elbow forms the fulcrum of this exercise.

❷ ◁ Using a rotating action towards the outer part of your body, start to turn your fingertips in a downwards, circular motion. Then rotate your wrist about your elbow. Apply gentle pressure on the left hand to stretch the forearms, elbows and wrists. This relaxes the elbow and enhances flexibility of your lower arm. Repeat this exercise 2 to 3 times each side.

EXERCISE 2 – *Preparation for* sankyo *wrist techniques. Sankyo is a painful, but very effective wrist restraint.*

❶ △ Turn your left hand slightly inwards with your fingertips pointing towards your abdomen. This exercise has been developed in preparation for a technique known as *sankyo*. Prepare for the grip, using your right hand to turn your left hand inwards so that your knuckles are facing towards your chest.

❷△ Twist and turn your wrist to the left side to ensure maximum rotation of the lower arm and wrist. Release and repeat the exercise with the right hand. Your hand needs to be well drawn in and move in an inward, circular motion, to apply pressure on the ligaments in your forearm.

EXERCISE 4 – *This exercise is in preparation for the technique called* nikkyo *or "wrist-in turn".*

△ Cover the back of your left hand with your right hand. Pull in towards the solar plexus area. This exercise assists in loosening and strengthening the wrist area.

Exercise | Spiritual development

Aikido seeks to develop your spiritual side in order to promote your inner calm. The attainment of inner tranquility is fundamental to clearing and focusing the mind in all aspects of life. The following exercises seek to bring together the qualities of correct breathing, known as *kokkyo* (breath power), as part of the spiritual development of aikido.

ROWING EXERCISE – *TORIFUNE* – *Think of this rowing exercise as a way of "rowing" from this world to the next. The exercise starts slowly but, towards the end of the session, the tempo is increased as you move "closer to Utopia". In the physical dimension it is used as a centering technique to instill a feeling of good body posture and, by emphasizing hip movement, to increase the awareness of your own centre of gravity.*

❶ ◁ Stand in the upright posture known as *migi hanmi* – right foot forward. *Migi* is Japanese for "right" and *hanmi* means "posture". Lean forwards and feel a sense of pressure from the hips. Fully extend your hands and start a rowing action, as if in a boat with oars.

❷ ◁ Pull back your fists to your hips, with your elbows tucked in, and around 70 per cent of your weight on your rear leg. Repeat this action several times and then change leg positions and repeat. Breathing is very important in this exercise – exhale on the forward movement using the sound of "*hei*" and, as you move back with your fists to the hip position, inhale, then exhale, using a "*ho*" sound. This is a low sound, which comes from the pit of the abdomen.

CALMING EXERCISE – *FURITAMA* – *This exercise is designed to bring an overall feeling of calmness to the body.*

❶ △ Stand in a relaxed position with your feet a shoulder-width apart. Fully extend your arms at the sides, palms upwards and with fingers open – as if grasping energy from the universe. Keep your eyes closed to maintain a feeling of calm.

❷ △ Bring your hands together, palms touching, above your head, with your fingers pointing upwards.

❸ △ Next, bring your hands down in front of your body in the region of your lower abdomen. Clasp your hands together, using a shaking motion, as if vibrating a heavy ball in your abdomen. The shaking movement is designed to help disperse the energy you have throughout your body.

Exercise | Breathing

In aikido, correct breathing not only oxygenates the blood, but also stimulates certain internal organs. In order to generate *kokkyo* (breath power), it is necessary to breathe deeply, with the emphasis on abdominal expansion and contraction, as opposed to simply breathing through the chest cavity. The following demonstrates just one of the many techniques we can learn.

❶ ◁ Stretch your body, arms above your head, with your palms facing upwards. As you perform this exercise, breathe in through your nose, imagining the breath going up to the top of your head, down the spine and into the centre of your abdomen. Perform this exercise slowly and deeply, as if there were a coil within your body, gradually unwinding. It may help to imagine that you have a spring in your abdomen – as you inhale it is compressed and as you exhale it is allowed to expand.

❷ △ As you bend at the waist to lower your body, begin to exhale.

❸ △ Try to touch your knees with your forehead by clasping the back of your ankles to pull your body inwards. At the same time, exhale fully. As you return to the original standing position, inhale then exhale as you remain standing. Repeat this exercise several times.

Exercise | Back-stretching

Traditional aikido places great emphasis on having a supple spine. Back-stretching exercises are, therefore, very much a part of every warm-up and cool-down session. The following exercises focus primarily on back-stretching and have benefits for the whole body in terms of flexibility and fitness.

EXERCISE 1 – *Sotai-dosa (paired practice) back-stretching exercise.*

1 △ With feet shoulder-width apart, step forward into a natural right foot posture. As your partner takes hold of your wrists, extend your fingers and imagine you have a sword in your hands.

2 △ Using a circular motion, bring your right foot forwards and upwards, approximately 45 degrees in front of your partner. Twist your body 180 degrees with the feeling that you are now cutting with the sword as you turn to the rear. You will then be back-to-back with your partner.

3 ◁ Keep turning your body as if you are cutting with your sword across your partner's throat. Both partners need to work together to gain benefit from this exercise. Hold your partner in this position for 5–6 seconds and then change roles, before repeating the exercise to the opposite side.

▽ Your partner at this point should have a very arched back and be gripping your arm for support, as you can see below, in this alternative view of this same position.

EXERCISE 2 – Ganseki otoshi *(head over heels throw). This is an effective defence used as a back-stretching exercise.*

❶ △ Your partner moves in with an overhead strike to the top of your head. Come in to meet the strike with your right forearm. In this exercise, this is purely a defensive move, although the defender treats the strike as a committed attack.

❷ △ With your right foot forward, bring your left foot around and pivot on the ball of your right foot so that you are now behind your partner. Maintain arm contact as you prepare for the next stage.

❸ △ Take hold of your partner's collar at the back of the neck with your left hand, while pushing your right arm and elbow into the centre of your partner's back in preparation for the lift.

❹ △ Once you feel secure, with your arm well positioned in the small of your partner's back, drop into a very low posture, keeping your knees well bent. *Note: while this is only an exercise, it must be performed with care and caution at all stages.*

❺ ▷ Gently lift your partner off the floor so that their body is completely arched and relaxed. The purpose of this exercise is to offer your partner support by using your body underneath to lift and gently bounce as your partner relaxes. Hold this position for approximately 15–20 seconds then change sides and repeat once only.

❶ △ Your partner approaches from the rear and grabs hold of both of your wrists.

❷ △ Start to move by bringing your right arm directly above your head to pull your partner off balance.

❸ △ Turn completely around, moving towards your partner at the same time. You should now be facing your partner, who must still hold on to your wrists in preparation for the back-stretching exercise. It is important to work cooperatively to ensure the success of this exercise.

❹ △ Your partner's back will now be fully arched. Their body must stay relaxed. You must maintain a good, strong, upright posture in order to support your partner. *Note: maintain this position for no more than 10 seconds, especially when first learning this exercise. Gently allow your partner to move back to an upright position.*

EXERCISE 4 – *Another defence technique that can be used as a warm-up stretch for your partner.*

❶ △ Your partner takes hold of both of your wrists.

❷ △ Start to move in with your right foot, pulling your left foot inwards. At the same time, bring your right arm across your partner's chest, keeping your left arm fully extended and forward.

❸ ▷ Slowly push your arm downwards and across the area of your partner's neck. With the twist of your hips, by following this movement through, you can throw your partner. *Note: do not apply any pressure to the neck. This is an exercise purely to promote suppleness. Hold position for 5–10 seconds and repeat.*

Technique | Basic stance and posture

Aikido adopts the back triangle stance (*ura-sankaku*). The triangle shape is achieved by the positioning of the feet. This is the only posture from which the *tanden* (centre) can be held effectively when executing a technique, and from where rapid movement in any direction is possible.

❶ ◁ Align the heels of both feet, with your front foot facing forwards and slightly outwards, and your rear foot at an angle of 60 degrees. Bend your knees slightly and place about 60 per cent of your weight on your front leg. Keep your hands in the guard position to protect your body. This stance is known as *hanmi* (half stance).

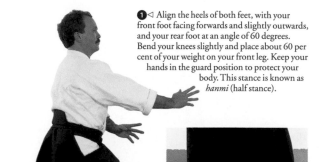

△Ideally the heel of your front foot must be in line with the heel of your rear foot, in a triangular shape, like being on a tight rope.

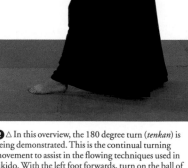

❷ △ In this overview, the 180 degree turn (*tenkan*) is being demonstrated. This is the continual turning movement to assist in the flowing techniques used in aikido. With the left foot forwards, turn on the ball of the foot and bring the left foot around circularly.

△ Use a pivoting action to bring your left leg around in a circular motion towards the rear. This detailed close-up shows the correct feet position in preparation for the turn.

❸ ◁After pivoting, you will have smoothly turned completely around 180 degrees and will be facing in the opposite direction, with your right foot forward. Depending on whether you use the front or rear foot to initiate the movement will dictate which foot is forward on the final turn. Qualified supervision is required to practise.

NOTE
In aikido each partner is referred to as the *uke* or *tori*. The **uke** is the initial attacker who will "receive" the restraint or throw and the *tori* will "execute" the defensive technique .

Technique | Standing

Learning to defend from a variety of different angles is important. The following demonstrates the use of the wrist technique *sankyo*, during an attack called *yoko menuchi* – a roundhouse strike to the side of the head. This is a very effective restraint from which it is difficult for an aggressor to escape.

2 ▽ Using a large circular motion, step through with your left foot as if walking through your partner. Keep the upward circular motion going, and then pull your partner's right hand back with your right hand, ensuring that their palm is facing outwards, while applying pressure on their elbow joint with your left hand.

1 △ Your partner comes in with a *yoko menuchi* technique, which is similar to a bottle being swung around to the side of the head. You defend yourself against the attack by coming in to meet the technique and deflect it with your left hand, while placing your right hand in front of your partner's face as a distraction.

3 ◁ Step through with your left leg, into a deep stance. Change the grip by moving your left hand down to take a secure hold of your partner's right hand. Keep your body in close and lean forwards to ensure that your left shoulder is well in to the side of your partner. From here there are a variety of final techniques that can be applied to fully restrain.

Technique | *Ikkyo – Suwari-waza*

Ikkyo is the first principle in arm pinning techniques and mastery of it is required to understand subsequent methods and skills. It can be practised from any attack, whether kneeling (*suwari-waza*), as shown here, or standing (*tachi-waza*). Sitting and standing practice is referred to as *hanmi-handachi*.

① ▷ Your partner comes at you with an overhead strike to the top of your head. This is known as *shomen uchi* and can be executed with the open hand or with the use of a weapon such as a knife. Defend by using both hands in an upwards motion to meet the attacking arm. *Note: use minimal aggression – a flowing motion and circular action have more impact than a static movement.*

② ▽ The twisting and turning action of the movement will help to bring your partner to the floor. This demonstrates the force that can be successfully applied. *Note: it is important that your partner is well experienced in break-falling techniques, to perform the technique as depicted. If not, you must gently position your partner in preparation for the final restraining technique.*

③ △ The final pin is effective by holding above the elbow and wrist, making sure the arm is slightly higher than the shoulder. Push from the centre of gravity with a twisting action.

Technique | *Kotegaeshi*

Kotegaeshi (wrist-out turn) is a basic technique whereby the defender places his hand on the back of the attacker's hand and applies pressure in two ways – inwards to break the power in attacking wrist and arm, and outwards to cause the attacker to fall onto their back, prior to restraining.

2 ◁ Take hold of your partner's right wrist to bring her arm down towards your thighs. This is important, since this is part of a flowing, continuous movement that uses your partner's energy as well as your own.

3 ▽ Continue the circular movement in the opposite direction. The complete motion is almost like a figure eight, with your partner's fingers being bent back to face downwards.

1 △ As your partner moves in with the overhead attack, move in and underneath to meet the attack with your right forearm. Your left arm is to the side and ready to go over your partner's right arm. Start to draw your hands downwards towards your partner's wrist, simultaneously keeping the momentum of the circle going towards you, and prepare to swing your body round to the left side.

4 ▷ Move through with your left knee, maintaining a firm grip on your partner's wrist, while securing pressure on your partner's elbow joint. As your partner feels they are about to hit the floor, continue the circle towards your left side by bringing your left knee around and both hands downwards in the same direction. This will force your partner to roll onto their back.

△ A locking technique showing the firm control required to immobilize your partner.

Technique | *Kata dori*

Kata dori is a shoulder grasp with one hand while the aggressor strikes with the other or kicks. The grasping arm is stretched sideways to take the attacker's balance prior to execution of the technique. This technique is also a useful self-defence move against clothing being grabbed in the street.

❶ △ Your partner moves in and grabs you by the sleeve.

❷ ▷ Bring your right hand across your partner's attacking right arm. Start to move your body forwards with your left foot so that you can start to pull your partner off balance.

△ To move into step 3, bring your left hand under your partner's right elbow, with your palm open and fingers upright. Bring your right hand under their wrist to apply a large circular forwards and downwards motion so that their right arm is in front of you.

△ To apply this alternative arm lock, place your left hand on your partner's elbow and your right hand on her wrist. Next, with your right hand, twist your partner's right hand with their fingers pointing away from you. Maintain pressure on the elbow joint.

△ A wrist technique such as *sankyo* can also be applied as an alternative manoeuvre. Pull your partner's left arm backwards and inward. This will cause the ligaments and nerves to twist.

3 ◁ Continue to step forwards to completely take your partner off balance and slide your left arm down towards their right thumb. This is in preparation to secure a wrist lock.

4 △ Apply a wrist lock by placing your left hand on the elbow joint to secure the restraint.

5 △ Maintain the wrist lock by taking hold of your partner's hand. Make sure their fingers are facing upwards.

6 ▷ Using a circular motion, bring your partner's right hand upwards, with her fingers pointing towards your face. This technique will cause discomfort and she may well come up on to her toes to release the pressure. This demonstrates that the technique has been correctly applied. Do not continue to apply pressure and release the hold as soon as possible.

Technique | Rear defence

Aikido incorporates defence from any attack, including holds or strikes from behind. Attacks from the rear are called *ushiro waza* (rear techniques). The following is an example of *ushiro katate dori kubeshime* (rear strangle with one hand held), demonstrating the effective use of posture and stance to support the technique being applied.

❶ ▷ You are grabbed from behind, around the throat, by your partner's right arm, and your left wrist is held by their left hand.

❷ △ Step back with your left leg, going underneath the attack. Project your energy forwards to take your attacker off balance. From this position a variety of techniques can be applied, as in step 3 below.

❸ △ In this case, apply a wrist lock to restrain your partner. Place your left hand on top of their left hand and your right hand on their wrist. Pull her hand to your chest and twist her fingers outwards, towards your right side. This action will cause the ligaments and nerves to twist.

Technique | Front defence

The following demonstrates a defence against a two-handed strangle known as *udehishige* (arm smashing). This technique is one of the few transmitted from *daito-ryu-ju-jitsu* that has not been changed from its original form. The founder modified many of the original techniques to incorporate his philosophy of *"aiki"*, making them less destructive.

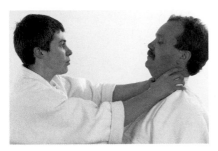

❶ △ You are grabbed by your partner around the throat from the front. Ideally, you need to start your defensive action before the grab is secure, but if this is not possible there are various techniques taught in aikido to defeat the attack.

❷ ▷ Practise this technique with the aim of taking hold of your partner's right wrist before contact is made.

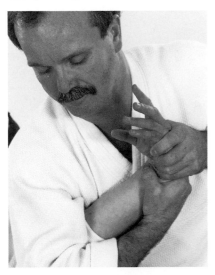

❸ △ Once you have grabbed your partner, bring your right arm over her arm, at the same time grabbing her right hand with your left hand and, simultaneously, twisting your body forwards to execute a lock on her arm, wrist and hand. The tips of your partner's fingers need to be pointing backwards.

❹ ▷ Twist your body around as far as you can away from your partner. Keep the lock close to your body, however. This will ensure an effective restraint or, alternatively, you can release your partner, projecting her forwards as part of a take down technique. Once the armlock is established, apply pressure by twisting your hips to the right.

Technique | Women's self-defence

While this section is referred to as "women's self-defence", the same techniques are also used by men and children. Aikido, being based upon the principle of the circle and using the aggressor's force, means that regardless of the size of the aggressor, your body weight can be used to maximize your advantage.

SHIHO NAGE – Four-direction throw – once the elbow is controlled it is possible to throw an attacker forwards, backwards or to either side.

❶ △ The attacker pins the arms to the side from behind, affecting a hug. Step forwards and extend your arms outwards in order to avoid encirclement.

❷ △ Extend your arms outwards with your right arm moving upwards and left arm in a downwards direction. With your left hand take hold of your partner's left wrist.

❸ △ Maintain the circular momentum as you step back and throw your partner forwards. Keep your body calm and extend your energy as you move through and throw.

IRIMI NAGE – This technique means "entering body throw".

❶ △ An aggressor tries to deliver a punch to your chest or stomach. Side-step to your left with your left foot to avoid it and deflect the aggressor's right-handed punch. This is an evasive technique. You can use your left hand (palm heel) to deflect the attack, but the most important thing is to move your body to the side so that you can deliver an immediate counter-attack. Once you have avoided the attack, bring your right hand up and across in a large circular action as you step through with your right foot. Simultaneously, bring your right arm under the aggressor's jaw line in preparation for a throw.

❷ △ Moving through, well into the aggressor's space, and breaking his posture, will cause him to lose balance and succumb to your technique. This requires minimal force but needs calmness, a flowing action, good timing and continuous movement.

ADVANCED
Technique | Self-defence against a knife

The category for knife defences is known as *tanto* or *tanken dori*. The aikido principle is still to evade the attack and use the aggressor's force against them. The knife is kept at a distance, while the flowing defensive manoeuvres are applied, utilizing the aggressor's energy to work in your favour.

CAUTION

When learning defences against a weapon attack it is vital to have qualified supervision and to practise in a safe environment. Never practise with a real weapon when you are learning, especially in the early stages. Wooden or plastic knives are ideal, but you still need to treat them with respect – any item can be dangerous if it is used incorrectly.

1 ▷ As the aggressor comes in with a right-handed knife attack to your stomach area, move to your left and block the strike with the outside edge of your hand. If, however, the attacker is left-handed, it would be more appropriate to move to your right. Bring the left foot forwards into a movement known as *irimi tenkan*, which is a 180-degree turn. It requires you to move in towards your opponent, turning your body, and the circular action and the physical movement will bring your opponent with you. You are turning outside your opponent's attacking energy, which is the principle of *tenkan*.

2 △ Seize the attacker's wrist with your left hand and take hold of his sleeve with your right hand – take hold of his arm if no clothing is available to grab. Move forwards with your left foot, pivoting on its ball, turn, and bring your right foot around as if doing a half-circle movement. Bring your left foot across, into an L-shaped position, and then step through with your right foot. This movement varies, depending on where you wish to manoeuvre your opponent.

3 △ Twist underneath the attacking arm and into a large circular movement, using your hands to take the aggressor off balance. As the aggressor enters into your movement, he is spun around – an action responsible for many of the dynamic throws employed in aikido. The force of the fall should ensure that he drops the knife. If appropriate, you could also apply a restraining hold, depending on the circumstances. If the attacker still has the knife, apply a further restraint to remove the weapon.

ADVANCED

Technique | Throwing – Nage waga

The following shows one of the basic throwing techniques to be found in aikido called *kaiten-nage*. As with all aikido styles, *kaiten-nage* seeks to develop the skills of both practitioners. The defender is learning the mechanics of the movement, as the partner also learns to use their agility to roll out of the throwing technique.

KAITEN-NAGE – *Objective is to spin your partner on to his back.*

As with all advanced techniques, especially throwing, it is very important for both partners to be experienced in break-falling before attempting any of these techniques.

❶ ▷ An aggressor comes in with a punch to
your solar plexus. You side-step and block
with your right arm, bringing your left hand
across to the back of the aggressor's neck. This
technique is called *kaiten-nage*, which means
"spin throw".

❷ △ Next, pull the aggressor's head down towards the floor with your left hand, while simultaneously pushing the aggressor's left arm upwards with your right hand. *Note: keep an upright, well-centred posture.*

❸ ▷ Finally, apply a throwing technique by pushing the aggressor's left arm forwards.

ADVANCED
Technique | Weapons

The following are some of the moves and techniques practised when using weapons such as the *bokken* and *jo*. Various *kata* (sequences of set moves) are taught, with and without a training partner, not only to develop skills in the use of weapons, but also to give a greater understanding of posture, timing and applications of *ma-ai* (combative distance).

❶ △ As the attacker thrusts with a *bokken*, the defender comes up underneath with their *bokken* to block the oncoming attack, prior to cutting the aggressor.

❷ △ The defender brings the *bokken* around his head and strikes the aggressor on the side of the neck.

▷ Demonstrating, using the *jo*, a technique called *otoshi tsuki* (meaning "drop thrust").

Exercise | Cool-down

Aikido practitioners believe it is important to cool down at the end of a session. One partner takes the other on to their back and gently extends upwards and outwards – the idea being to relax worked muscles and stretch the spine, to prevent stiffness ensuing after practice. The following moves demonstrate just two of a variety of body-relaxing exercises.

COOL-DOWN 1 – Haishin undo *(back stretching)*

1 ◁ Your partner takes hold of both your wrists.

2 ▷ Turn underneath and completely around, while your partner maintains a hold on your wrists, so that you are now back to back.

3 ▷ Drop your body down and place your buttocks well under your partner's buttocks in preparation for the lift. Lift your partner up and across your back, stretching your arms forwards. It is important that your partner totally relaxes while you gently stretch forward to loosen their spine. *Note: this exercise must not be performed if either of you have any back problems. If in doubt, consult a doctor.*

COOL-DOWN 2 – *Another interesting, unique technique in aikido is using the* bokken *in the cool-down exercises.*

❶ △ A similar cool-down technique uses the *bokken*. Stand facing each other in the standard *hanmi* posture. Your partner takes hold of your right wrist with both hands.

❷ △ Turn to the side with your right foot and pivot completely around on your left foot in an anticlockwise (counterclockwise) direction by bringing your right leg to the rear. At the same time, raise the *bokken* as if to start to cut.

❸ ▷ Continue the turn so that you are now facing the opposite direction and bring the *bokken* above your head as you turn. This will lift your partner and bring her across your back. Hold for 15 to 20 seconds and change sides. Perform this exercise slowly and carefully.

JU-JITSU

Ju-jitsu is an effective self-defence system used extensively by the military and police forces around the world. Special features of the art include defences against knife attacks and immobilizing techniques. Another unique skill taught to highly qualified practitioners is the art of resuscitation. This technique, known as *kuatsu,* was developed on the battlefield where, following the delivery of a non-fatal ju-jitsu technique, rather than deliver a final killing blow, a Japanese *samurai* would revive the injured enemy for questioning.

柔術

JU-JITSU

history *and* philosophy

The art of ju-jitsu is interpreted as being the "science of softness". Translated literally, *ju* means "gentle" or "soft" and *jitsu* means "art". While referred to as "a gentle art" some of the techniques are, nevertheless, extremely dynamic in their delivery and would appear to be anything but soft.

There are many stories regarding the origins of ju-jitsu, dating as far back as the 8th century, with historical lines indicating roots even before the time of Christ. While some people claim that ju-jitsu originated in China, the ancient chronicles of Japan describe how, in AD 712, Tatemi Kazuchi threw Tatemi Nokami, like "throwing a leaf". Reference is also made in the *Nihon Sho-ki* chronicles to the Emperor Shuinjin holding a martial arts tournament to celebrate the seventh year of his reign in 23 BC. One of the bouts resulted in the death of a participant, a sumo wrestler, who was thrown to the ground and kicked by Nomino Sukume. These accounts provide evidence of early "empty-hand" techniques in Japan. There is also reference to ju-jitsu developing as an art from the work of a Buddhist monk, dating back to the 13th century. These ancient techniques were known as *kumi-tachi* (or *yawara*), which is described in the *Konjaku-monogatari*, a Buddhist work dating back to that time.

A few practitioners of ju-jitsu choose to keep alive the warrior spirit of the fighting techniques.

Another reference to a ju-jitsu-like form of combat is found in the 15th-century martial art tradition known as the katori-shinto ryu. It is believed, however, that ju-jitsu was brought to Japan by a Chinese monk called Chen Yuanein (1587-1671). So, although ju-jitsu is viewed today as a Japanese martial art, there is strong evidence pointing to Chinese origins.

While ju-jitsu was first practised in Japan by the *samurai*, followed by the *ninja*, it inevitably spread further afield and was, sadly, embraced by many of the bandits of the time.

Through this dubious association, ju-jitsu earned a poor reputation. It was during this time that Jiguro Kano developed the art of judo, meaning "the gentle way", from a combination of ju-jitsu techniques. His aim was to correct the reputation ju-jitsu had acquired as a deadly art through its connections with banditry.

What is ju-jitsu?

The central philosophy behind ju-jitsu is to conquer an opponent by any and all means – as long as minimal force

Ju-jitsu followers conform to a strict discipline – both mental and physical.

The essence of ju-jitsu is the power of resistance and effective timing.

only is used. Consequently, this precept demands from its followers a strict conformity to various disciplines – both mental and physical.

Physical fitness has always been a fundamental prerequisite for practitioners of ju-jitsu. A characteristic of this art involves strict moral and dietary regimes, which are seen as being necessary if one is to reach the highest level of perfection. It is therefore not surprising that, historically, many ju-jitsu masters withdrew to religious institutions, such as Buddhist or Shinto shrines.

Although the fundamental principle behind modern ju-jitsu as a self-defence art is to conquer an opponent using minimal force, the older art of ju-jitsu focused on literally annihilating the enemy, which led to the development of many dangerous and fatal techniques.

Warrior traditions

The *samurai* followed a strict code of discipline called the *bushido* – the "way of the warrior". This code included such concepts as loyalty, duty, obedience, honour and respect. The code influenced not just their behaviour in battle, but their daily lives, too. This would become the basis of the Zen Buddhist philosophy – reaching for salvation within, rather

than turning to a monument or god. The *samurai* believed that man could influence his own destiny, especially when faced with warfare and possible death – a concept which certainly appealed to them.

The traditional art of ju-jitsu is still carried on today by a minority of practitioners, who wish to keep alive the warrior spirit of the deadly fighting techniques of the art. They do not enter competitions and their only goal is the continuation of the mental, spiritual and physical purity of the art.

BENEFITS OF JU-JITSU

The principal benefits that derive from learning the art of ju-jitsu include:

• Fitness and flexibility
• Confidence and well-being
• Self-defence skills
• Assertiveness and awareness
• Stress reduction
• Comradeship
• Self-discipline and a positive attitude

clothing *and* equipment

In ju-jitsu students generally wear a white suit (*gi*) and a red belt. This depicts their beginner status. They will then follow the grade system, changing belt colours as they achieve each grade detailed below. When students attain their first black belt grade (1st-*dan* – *shodan*) their clothing is changed to a black jacket and white trousers, which become a blue jacket from 4th-*dan*. It is always important to ensure that the suit fits comfortably for safety and practicality. It is also necessary that students and instructors keep their suits in good repair and are always smart in appearance. Personal hygiene is very important, particularly when practising in close proximity with another partner. Practitioners must ensure that their nails are clean and short, that jewellery is removed and hair is tied back where appropriate. This is important, as there are many close proximity techniques in ju-jitsu, and this will avoid unnecessary injury. It is compulsory in this style of ju-jitsu for both men and women to wear groin protection (athletic cup) from the day they begin their training.

gi *top*

groin protection (athletic cup)

trousers

zori

Belt gradings

Grade	Belt
7th-*kyu*	White (red stripe)
6th-*kyu*	Yellow
5th-*kyu*	Orange
4th-*kyu*	Green
3rd-*kyu*	Blue
2nd-*kyu*	Purple
1st-*kyu*	Brown
Shodan-ho	Black and brown (provisional black)
1st–5th-*dan*	Black
6th-*dan* and upwards	Red and white

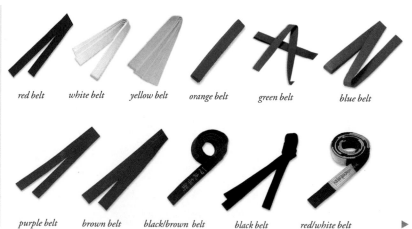

red belt   *white belt*   *yellow belt*   *orange belt*   *green belt*   *blue belt*

purple belt   *brown belt*   *black/brown belt*   *black belt*   *red/white belt*

Equipment

The *hojo jutsu* rope is unique to the art of ju-jitsu. It was originally used by the *samurai* to detain prisoners of war as part of their duty when they served as feudal police. Today, around the world, the *hojo jutsu* rope is still used by many police and special security forces to detain criminals, prisoners and terrorists. Below is a selection of the weapons used in ju-jitsu. There are many other weapons, such as the *hoko* and *yari* (spears), *naginata* (wooden staff) and *nunchaku* (small rice flail).

A hakama is also worn in ju-jitsu usually for the specific practise of certain techniques and for demonstrations.

jo

bo

kamma

sai

tanto

hojo jutsu *rope*

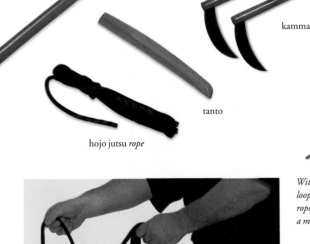

With a slipknot and loop, the hojo jutsu *rope is used mainly as a method of restraint.*

tonfa

Etiquette

Etiquette is important as a sign of respect to the spirit of the art (*shomen*), instructors, students and to the training environment (*dojo*). This form of etiquette is an integral part of the practice. The following demonstrates the kneeling bow (*rei*) followed by the standing bow, before commencing training.

KNEELING *REI* (BOW)

1 △ Lower yourself down on to your left knee with both hands towards your left hip. This position represents holding a sword as in the day of the Japanese *samurai*.

2 △ Take hold of your trousers with your right hand on your right knee. (This movement represents the *samurai* wearing the *hakama* – pleated trousers/skirt, and the need to slightly lift this garment before drawing the foot in.) Bring your right foot back so as not to compromise your stance in the event that you need to quickly respond to an attack.

3 △ Bring your right leg back so that you can lower your body to sit on both heels with your feet flat. Position your hands at the top of your thighs and keep your arms and shoulders relaxed. Make sure your knees are no more than two fists apart. It is disrespectful for your knees to be any wider than this. Place your hands on the tops of your thighs with your fingers pushed together. Continue to look forwards with your back and shoulders in an upright position. Although this is an assertive position, keep your body relaxed.

STANDING *REI* (BOW)

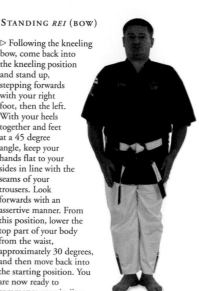

4 △ Prior to performing the *rei*, there is a rather more assertive posture in the form of a slight "snap" action. As you start to bow forwards, place your left hand to the front of your body. This depicts protecting the sword, which would be carried on the left side of the body. While being a sign of respect, it is also a sign of possible distrust. Overall, the etiquette needs to be performed smoothly and naturally.

5 △ Follow through with your right hand, making sure that your fingers and thumb touch to make a diamond shape – this is known as the *kongo zen* diamond. This side view of the bow shows the correct angle of the head, hands and feet.

▷ Following the kneeling bow, come back into the kneeling position and stand up, stepping forwards with your right foot, then the left. With your heels together and feet at a 45 degree angle, keep your hands flat to your sides in line with the seams of your trousers. Look forwards with an assertive manner. From this position, lower the top part of your body from the waist, approximately 30 degrees, and then move back into the starting position. You are now ready to commence your ju-jitsu practice.

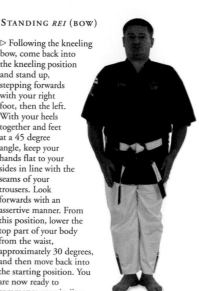

Exercise | Warm-up

It is very important to carry out appropriate warm-up exercises before beginning ju-jitsu practice. These usually consist of running around the outside of the *dojo* to loosen up your body and increase your heart rate, improving circulation. The running exercise can incorporate a variety of physical moves as part of the warm-up routine.

WARM-UP 1 – *This exercise will loosen your shoulder muscles and joints.*

❶ ◁ With feet a shoulder-width apart, rotate both your arms in a forwards, circular motion.

❹ ◁ Push your right arm upwards, as if to touch your left shoulder. This will apply gentle pressure to your elbow joint and increase suppleness. Repeat this movement with your left arm 2 or 3 times.

❷ △ Here you can see the arms going above the head, continuing the circular action to the rear and then returning to the start position. Use a large, circular action at a medium pace only. Repeat this exercise several times and then reverse the action so that your arms are moving backwards and then forwards.

❸ △ With your feet a shoulder-width apart, cross your arms in front of your body by bringing your left arm on top of your right arm.

❶ ◁ Stretch out your right hand in front of your body with your palm facing outwards. Keep your fingers tightly closed together and your thumb tucked in.

△ This close-up shows the correct position of your hands.

❷ ◁ With your left hand, take hold of the back of your right hand. Ensure your left thumb is placed on top of your right hand. Again, your fingers need to be pushed together.

❸ ▷ Pull your right hand in towards your nose or chin area. This will stimulate a pulling sensation to the forearm muscles and tendons. Maintain pressure with a slight twisting action. Relax and repeat 3 or 4 times. Repeat with the left hand.

▶

1 ◁ Standing with your feet a shoulder-width apart, place your hands on your hips and start to rotate them in a clockwise direction. Make sure you keep your feet firmly flat on the ground and that you are working the middle part of your body. This exercise is particularly good for the base of the spine and pelvis.

2 ▷ With your feet together, bend your knees. Place the palm of your hands on top of your knees and push in a circular clockwise direction. Repeat several times. Then repeat the exercise in an anticlockwise (counterclockwise) direction. Perform this movement slowly and gently to increase the suppleness of your knees, without causing cartilage problems.

3 △ Stretch your left leg out to the side, heel on the floor and with your toes raised, and lower your body towards the right by bending your right knee about 90 degrees. Keep your left leg straight. You will feel a stretching sensation on the hamstrings of your left leg. Repeat this exercise on the opposite side, once only.

4 △ Start with feet shoulder-width apart and step forwards. Place your hands on your hips, turn to your right and push forwards with your right knee. Ensure that your left leg remains straight with your heel firmly on the floor. Push forwards with your hips to stretch the tendons of the left leg. Your chest should be upwards and forwards, chin up and eyes looking forwards. Repeat this exercise to the left side once only.

WARM-UP 4 – *The following exercise will strengthen and condition different areas of the feet, making them more supple.*

1 ◁ Stand with your feet a shoulder-width apart and turn them outwards, as if rocking on the outside edges of your feet.

▽ Roll on to the sides of your feet as shown here, as far as you comfortably can.

2 ◁ Pull your knees inwards and transfer your weight on to the inside edges of your feet in a rolling action.

▽ Roll on to your instep.

3 ◁ Straighten your legs and roll your weight forwards, so that you are balancing on the balls of your feet.

▽ Keep your heels well raised for maximum benefit.

4 ◁ Roll your weight backwards so you are balancing on your heels. Keep your arms forward to maintain good balance. Repeat 3 or 4 times each side.

▽ Keep toes curled upwards and off the floor.

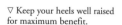

Technique | Blocking

There are various defensive techniques in ju-jitsu that involve blocking, covering the head, upper body and lower body. The following techniques demonstrate some of these blocks. There are comparative blocking techniques which can be found in other martial arts such as karate and tae kwondo. The blocks here are particular to ju-jitsu.

S BLOCK – *Swan neck block*

1 ◁ Face your partner with your left hand forward, assuming a guard position.

2 ▷ As your partner moves towards you with a round-house punch (right hook) to the head, turn your body to the left and bring your left arm forwards through the centre of your body and out towards the left. Following this S block, you would make a strike to the face, body or groin area. Make sure that your palm is facing downwards with your fingers locked together. Repeat this exercise, reversing roles with your partner.

3 ▷ As you move through with the S block, prepare your right hand, ready to strike your partner.

◁ This close-up demonstrates the effectiveness of the S block.

4 ▽ With your right hand palm heel, aim to strike towards your partner's chin, focusing your strike at least 3–5 in (7.5–13 cm) away from your partner's chin. This is important to maintain safety. *Note: blocking will incur contact, but be sensible in the delivery of your techniques.*

CROSS BLOCK – *Defending the middle to upper part of the body.*

❶ △ Move into a formal posture (left-hand fighting stance) with about three-quarters of your weight on your back leg. This enables you to use your front leg in a rapid kicking technique, should this be necessary – or any other defensive technique.

❸ ◁ Grab your partner's right wrist and prepare to strike. It is important to adopt a strong posture, while you bring your fist across your body, before delivering the strike.

❹ ▽ Strike your partner in the floating rib with the side of your right fist (hammer fist). Your fingers should be tightly clenched with your thumb locked over the top of your fingers.

▷ Maintain a secure grip while striking.

❷ ◁ As your partner moves towards you with a right-fist strike at your head, step across and block with both hands. Ensure that your left hand is in the "open-hand" position.

▽ Keep looking at your partner when performing your techniques and do not drop your guard.

❺ △ Depending on the situation, you can now apply an arm lock. When doing this it is important to aim for the weak areas of your partner's body. Your right arm must clasp your partner's right arm just above the elbow joint, your left hand securing his wrist. *Note that your right foot is positioned behind your partner's right foot. This gives good posture and stance and ensures that your partner cannot follow through with any further movements.*

ADVANCED
Technique | Shoulder lock

The following demonstrates a combination of blocking, striking and locking techniques that can be used to restrain an aggressor. This sequence of moves is typical of many ju-jitsu techniques, which combine the hard and soft concept. Each move in itself may be applied from different directions and can have several variations.

1 ◁ Stand opposite your partner in the formal stance position with your fists raised.

2 ▷ Move into the back stance, with about 75 per cent of your weight on your rear leg, and prepare to block, using a downward circular motion, with the palm of your hand. Your fingers should be straight and locked together, with your thumb bent and locked inside the hand. Your left hand blocks your partner's right arm, striking his inner forearm. Have your right fist ready to make a counter-strike.

3 △ Strike at your partner's floating rib with your right fist. Use hip momentum when delivering the strike.

△ Close-up of the strike into the neck area.

4 ▷ Raise your right arm in a large circular motion to chop into your partner's neck, thus enabling you to eventually roll him down and apply a shoulder lock.

5 ◁ To develop this technique to a more advanced stage, apply a restraining technique by moving your left arm under your partner's right arm. *Note the posture and bent knees.*

6 ▷ Go with the restraint until you lock your partner well into your body. His right arm is now secured against the left side of your neck and both your hands are clasped above his right shoulder. Keep a low posture (horse stance) and keep your partner well secured and close to your body.

7 ◁ Bring your right arm up in front of your forehead, almost as if you are saluting.

8 ▷ Take hold of your partner's right wrist with your right hand and push his fingers outwards.

9 △ Continue to push his fingers and arm away from you. From this particular position you could then keep the momentum going and throw your partner, creating distance and giving you time to escape.

10 △ Alternatively, to restrain your partner, bring his right arm across his back in a figure-four arm lock.

Technique | Passive defensive stance

The purpose of the passive defensive stance is to lull an attacker into a false sense of security. This is a combination of defusion skills using verbal communication and body language to throw the aggressor off guard. These are particularly advanced techniques requiring qualified supervision. The following demonstration is intended as a guide only.

❶ ◁ Step back with your left leg into the passive defensive stance. About 75 per cent of your weight should be on this leg. Bring your hands up level with your partner's eyes, palms facing forwards and fingers splayed. This depicts the body language of a submissive, calming nature. You are trying to communicate "I don't want any trouble".

❷ ▷ As your partner moves in and grabs your clothing, take hold of his right wrist with your left hand. Secure your partner's right hand with your left hand. Maintain a good, strong stance.

❸ △ Using your right hand, flick at your partner's eyes to distract him.

△ This close-up shows the correct position, necessary for the securing hand grip.

❹ ▷ Bring your right arm up and over your partner's right arm. Keep his right wrist firmly secured with your left hand.

5 △Push through with your right arm under your partner's right elbow, in order to trap his arm.

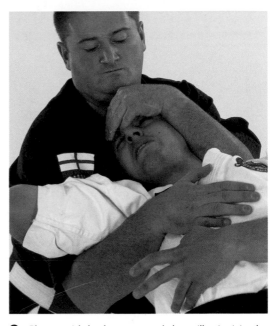

6 △ Place your right hand on your partner's chest, still maintaining the arm lock.

7 ◁ Bring your partner down to the floor by twisting his body in towards your chest. Ensure that your right arm is firmly placed on his chest, with the left hand restraining his forehead. It is important that you keep your partner as close to your body as possible in order to maintain control.

8 ◁ In a self-defence situation you may feel it necessary to strike in order to incapacitate an aggressor. One option is to strike with the knife edge of your hand into the groin area.

9 △ Alternatively, if you are an experienced practitioner and there is no danger from other quarters, you may wish to restrain an aggressor until assistance arrives.

Technique | Wrist defence

The following demonstrates one defence against a wrist attack, with the aim of countering the aggressor's initial attack and turning this to your advantage. Again, the combination of hard and soft is demonstrated by the use of wrist control (soft) and by striking techniques (hard).

1△ Your partner moves in and grabs your wrists. Maintain your distance and move into a formal posture in preparation to defend.

2△ With an open hand, push downwards and forwards.

3△ Turn your wrist like a corkscrew against your partner's thumb, pushing your right hand straight down. Make sure to keep a deep, low stance for stability.

4△ Bring your hand right back, ready to strike with the back of your hand to the area of your partner's groin.

5▷ Strike your partner's groin area with the back of your right hand.

6△ Take hold of your partner's elbow with your right hand.

7△ Your left hand begins to roll outwards from your partner's grip.

8△ Twist your left hand in an inwards and outwards circular action so that it rotates your wrist and is freed from the grip.

9△ While holding on to your partner's right arm with your right hand at the elbow joint, prepare for a left-hand palm heel strike. Still holding your partner's elbow joint, release your left hand in preparation to strike.

10△ Strike your partner in the face with the heel of your open hand.

11 △ Overview of the technique showing your partner starting to move backwards. Dependent upon the force and angle of the strike, your partner, if an aggressor, would either fall to the floor or stagger backwards.

Technique | Elbow restraint

The following defence could be used against a variety of attacks, such as a push or a grab to the chest. Dependent upon the circumstances, you may prefer to restrain your opponent, rather than strike or throw. Restraining the arm, by applying pressure to the elbow, can be particularly effective, as demonstrated below.

1 △ Your partner moves in to push you in the chest by placing his hand on the region of your solar plexus. This could also be a grab at your clothing.

2 △ Immediately place your hand across your partner's right hand, pinning it against your body. Always practise using your right and left hands in a self-defence situation.

3 △ Place your hand firmly across your partner's hand to prevent him grabbing you while you begin to apply the elbow restraint.

4 △ Place your left hand behind your partner's elbow while maintaining your grip on his hand. Push in from his elbow towards the centre of your body to apply a wrist lock.

5 ▷ Continue pushing inwards and upwards. This will cause an aggressor extreme pain, as well as lifting him on to his toes and unbalancing him.

Technique | Defence from rear stranglehold

It is important to cover all eventualities and attacks from different positions. The following looks at one technique which can be applied against a rear stranglehold. The intention could be to pull you back, so the following demonstrates the use of the body position to minimize the attack in preparation to strike.

❶ ◁ Your partner grabs you around the throat, either to pull you back or to try to strangle you.

❷ ▷ Turn into a low horse stance position by jumping half a turn to your right. With your left hand open, defend your head area with a palm heel facing towards your partner. Close the fingers of your right hand to make a fist, in preparation to strike your partner.

❸ ◁ Strike your partner with a hammer fist to his floating rib.

Technique | Tactical search technique

The following arrest and restraint technique is used when you attempt to apprehend an aggressor who may be attacking you or another individual. This particular technique is mainly used by the armed forces and police, especially in riot situations. In view of its complexity, this technique requires qualified supervision and tuition.

❶ △ As you come up behind the aggressor, grab the back of his clothing at the base of his neck, with your left hand. Keep your distance to prevent rear attack such as a kick.

❷ △ You then bring your right hand across the aggressor's throat in order to prevent any further assault.

❸ △ Place your left hand on the aggressor's forehead to secure a headlock. Note that the aggressor is being pulled backwards in order to upset his balance.

❹ △ Now step back and go down on to your left knee, ensuring that the head lock is still securely in place. Your right leg should be jutting out with a 90-degree bend on your knee to ensure a good posture.

❺ △ Bring your right leg around the aggressor's right arm and pull it back to secure a further restraint lock.

❻ △ Kneel to secure the arm lock. Ensure that your body weight is leaning over the opponent for maximum control. Make the arm lock close to the body ensuring that the aggressor cannot manoeuvre his way out of the technique.

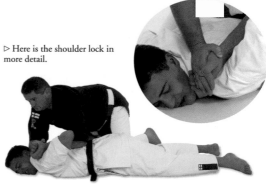

▷ This close-up shows how to hold the aggressor's head and wrist in place.

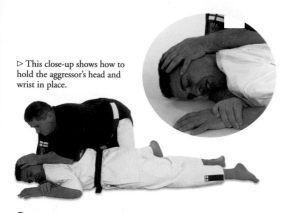

❼△ Roll the aggressor around on to his front, keeping the head lock as secure as possible. Release your right hand and take hold of the aggressor's left wrist, with your left hand securely on top of his head in the ear and temple region. Lean across the back of the aggressor so that your body weight makes an effective restraint.

▷ Here is the shoulder lock in more detail.

❽△ Maintain a secure arm lock and place your right hand across the back of the aggressor's neck. Start to manoeuvre your body upwards in preparation for the next part of the restraint.

❾△ Bring your left knee across the upper part of the aggressor's body, maintaining the shoulder lock, and push his arm up his back, keeping your body weight slightly forward.

❿▷ Lift the aggressor's arm up his back to secure the restraint.

△ This shows the exact hand and arm positions.

⓫△ Bring the aggressor's left arm across the front of your body, and to your right side, to effect a locking action.

⓬△ At this point the aggressor is fully restrained and can be searched. A search could be carried out if, for example, you were the armed forces, police or security. Start in the area of his neck, working down his spine and into the rear of his waistband. Then search the inside and outside of his legs and groin and other areas of his body.

Technique | Knife defence

There are a variety of knife techniques practised in ju-jitsu. Unless extremely experienced and highly qualified, a dummy knife is always used for safety. Using a dummy knife assists the practitioner to get the feel of an aggressor who may use a weapon of any description. Such practice can enhance the reflexes in the event of a real knife threat.

ATTACK TO THE STOMACH – *Learning to develop body evasion skills against a weapon.*

❶△ An attacker draws his knife and threatens your stomach.

❷△ Breathe in and turn to your side, clasping the aggressor's knife hand close to the flat of your stomach.

❸ △ Draw your elbow back in to pull the aggressor off balance and to keep him close in to you.

❹◁ Strike to the aggressor's face, or any other part of his body that is accessible and vulnerable. This will disorientate the aggressor.

❺△ Now take a firm double-handed grip on the aggressor's knife hand and prepare to sweep through with your left leg.

6 △ As you sweep your left leg around, moving in towards the aggressor, keep the knife well away from your body. This is a flowing movement which prepares you for the take-down and restraint.

7 ▷ After the aggressor is on the floor, make sure that the knife is still well away from your body.

△ This is the same position from a different angle.

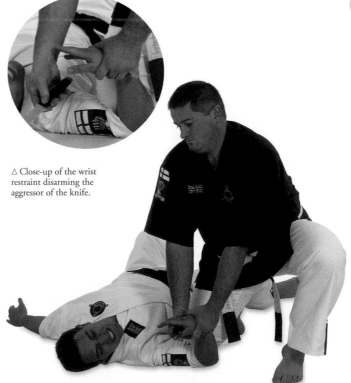

△ Close-up of the wrist restraint disarming the aggressor of the knife.

8 ▷ Apply a knee lock to the aggressor's elbow, maintaining the restraint until assistance arrives.

1 △ An aggressor moves in with a knife attack to your face. Step back and prepare to use a double-handed knife-edge block to the aggressor's right arm.

2 △ A double block requires both hands simultaneously striking the aggressor's attacking arm, to ensure the knife does not make contact. The use of both hands reinforces the ability to defend more effectively.

3 △ Keeping the knife attack away from your body, move in sideways and strike with your elbow to the aggressor's floating rib or solar plexus, depending on which is more accessible.

4 △ Feed your right hand through in a snake-like movement, bringing your hand over the aggressor's right wrist to create an arm lock (key lock).

5 ◁ Continue the momentum, keeping the knife well away from your body, and take the aggressor down to the floor. Apply a finishing strike, if necessary.

REAR ATTACK – *Learning how to escape from a rear-arm lock.*

❶△ An aggressor moves in and grabs you in an arm lock from behind.

❷△ Step forwards and simultaneously grab the aggressor's wrist to pull him off balance.

❸△ Strike with the knife edge of your left hand to the area of the aggressor's groin.

❹△ Following the groin strike, move under the aggressor's right arm in preparation to apply an arm lock. Keep both hands on the aggressor's right wrist to secure the restraint.

❺▷ Final technique demonstrating the application of a knee strike. In all cases, it is better to remain with a restraint, in view of the injuries which could be inflicted by using a "hard" strike.

Technique | Weapons

The following will give you an insight into some of the weapons (*kobojutsu*) and techniques used in ju-jitsu. Many of these weapons developed from practical farming tools used in everyday life many centuries ago. Qualified supervision and guidance must be sought when learning to use any weapons, and the following is for demonstration purposes only.

KAMMA – A kamma *is a type of sickle used to cut moss, hay and corn. It was developed centuries ago on the Japanese island of Okinawa.*

① △ This demonstrates the correct position in which to hold the *kamma*. Your body should be upright, your feet a shoulder-width apart and a *kamma* in each hand, in a crossed position, with the right hand uppermost.

② △ From here, move into a basic ready position by moving your right foot back into a long stance. Draw the right-hand *kamma* above your head, ready for a downwards strike, and hold the left-hand *kamma* in a forwards position as a defensive guard.

③ △ From this position, step forwards with your right foot, bringing your right hand down in a striking movement. Draw the left-hand *kamma* back ready for a follow-up strike if necessary.

④ ◁ Here, each *kamma* is being held in a blocking and striking position. The wooden part of the *kamma* could be used to deflect a strike, while being in the ready position for a follow-up strike.

⑤ ▷ The *kamma* was traditionally used by peasants against aggressors. This stance would be used to assist the cutting-up motion of the *kamma* towards an opponent's groin or lower body.

SAI – The sai *was mainly used as a defensive weapon against a sword, staff, stick or empty hand. It was a popular weapon used on the island of Okinawa.*

❷ ◁ Seen from the rear, the *sai* resting against the forearms and body are clearly visible.

△ A close-up of the *sai* demonstrates the fingers and thumb positions.

❶ △ Stand upright, feet a shoulder-width apart, with the *sai* resting invisibly against the inside of your forearm. When holding a *sai*, place your forefinger down its handle, with your other fingers wrapped around the outside, and your thumb tucked securely in on the inside.

❸ △ The *sai* being flicked inwards and outwards in a guard position, ready to guard and/or strike.

❹ △ The left-hand *sai* being used in a blocking position, while the one in the right hand is ready to strike.

TONFA – *The* tonfa *in Japan comes from the island of Okinawa, although it is thought to have originated in China. This baton-like implement was adapted from an agricultural tool used for grinding coal, maize and corn. Today it is used as an effective defensive, blocking and striking weapon.*

❶ ◁ In the starting position, stand upright with your feet a shoulder-width apart, and with the *tonfa* held hidden behind your forearms.

△ A close-up view of the correct grip on the *tonfa*.

❷ ▷ Note how the fingers and thumb are securely wrapped along the top part of the *tonfa*, so that it can be used as a blocking device, as well as pivoting through the hand as a striking weapon.

❸ ◁ This illustrates one of the positions adopted when up against an armed opponent. The left-hand *tonfa* is aligned against the edge of the forearm, where it can block any incoming blow.

❹ ▷ The right-hand *tonfa* is held flexibly, so that it can be twirled in a circular action to strike an opponent across the head.

BO – *The* bo *is a 6ft (2m) pole made of red or white oak (red here), about 1½in (3.5 cm) in diameter. Traditionally the* bo *developed from the staff (long pole) used by Buddhist priests.*

❶ ◁ This is the basic stance when using a *bo*, which should be held at the side of the body behind the right arm.

❷ ▷ Before striking with the *bo*, the practitioner steps back in a large circular motion.

JU-JITSU   TECHNIQUE

110

TANTO-JUTSU – *The tanto was used specifically to attack at close quarters the weak points of an opponent's armour. It could easily be concealed and was particularly popular with both men and women as a form of defence, to attack vulnerable areas at close range.*

JO – *The jo is similar to the bo, but it is much shorter – about 4 ft (1.2 m). It is also lighter and usually smaller in diameter. It is held in a similar fashion to the bo. There is a famous story of the jo being used to defeat a 16th-century samurai warrior called Musashi Miyamoto.*

△ This classic guard stance is used to deliver an attack with this short-range weapon.

△ The *jo* practitioner is seen here having delivered a strike to an opponent's throat or solar plexus. Note the stance, with his legs crossed over and knees bent for stability.

HOJO JUTSU – Hojo jutsu *is the traditional art of binding and restraining an aggressor on the battlefield. It is probably most commonly used today in security situations by the armed forces and military (it is a speciality of the Tokyo riot police). The purpose of the* hojo jutsu *techniques is to immobilize an opponent or aggressor until assistance arrives, or while they are being transported to a place of safety. The rope is traditionally 20 ft (6 m) long, which is twice the length of an adult martial arts belt (obi). It was traditionally worn around the waist and over the top of the armour. Today's martial arts practitioner would wear the* hojo jutsu *rope inside the jacket (dogi).*

❶ ◁ This picture portrays one of the *hojo jutsu* techniques to restrain an opponent. This is a specialized technique requiring considerable skill and special training.

❷ ▷ Here you can see that no knots are used – restraint is based on a series of loops and half hitches.

❸ ▷ This shows the correct method of holding the *hojo* rope. The remaining rope is kept within the *gi* top to conceal its true length.

JUDO

Judo, meaning "the gentle way", is regarded as a modern sport, deriving from ju-jitsu. The essence of judo is the skilful application of a combination of techniques, such as the power of resistance and effective timing. The main focus of judo, however, is the utilization of your opponent's body weight and strength against him or herself. There is some similarity in principle between judo and sumo wrestling, in that a small person can overcome a much larger opponent using skill, strategy and technique.

JUDO

history *and* philosophy

Professor Jiguro Kano, the founder of judo, graduated from the Imperial University of Tokyo, Japan, in 1881. He attended several ju-jitsu schools, seeking to develop a system of physical exercise. He adopted the best principles of each ju-jitsu system and called it judo, which, literally translated, means "gentle way". Kano's interpretation, however, was "maximum efficiency". He came to Europe in 1889 to spread the practice and philosophy of judo.

Kano envisaged judo as the development of a lifetime art, as opposed to a sport. Unusual for his time, he spoke perfect English and, breaking with Japanese tradition, his great respect for women prompted him to take on a female martial arts student, Sueko Ashiya. Criticisms were made that teaching women martial arts could lead to health problems because they had certain physical and other limitations that made them unsatisfactory students. Concerned with these comments, Kano undertook research into the impact that judo had on women, utilizing the knowledge of some of the leading medical experts of his day.

The research refuted his critics' claims concerning the negative impact of judo on women, and it was at about this time that Kano set up a *dojo* (training hall) for women in Koubun school, Tokyo. By 1935 judo was being successfully taught to women, especially in high school.

The first international judo tournament took place between Great Britain and France in 1947. Britain took the

Dismissing early doubts, judo was being taught to women by 1935.

title but, in 1951, the first European Championship was won by a French team. By 1956, judo was being taught in many Japanese schools. Unfortunately, Kano was not to witness any of this, since he died in1938, while at sea, returning from the Cairo International Olympic Conference. Some people claim that he was assassinated because of his actions and manifest sympathies towards the West.

It is worth bearing in mind that Kano did not create judo to be a public competition sport, and he felt strongly that it was a personal art to train the mind and body. He insisted that its mastery required an appreciation of the inherent philosophy that supports all aspects of judo. With this in mind, it is interesting to read the oath that all judo students at the *Kodukan dojo* (the name given by Kano to his *dojo*) must make on admission: "Once I have entered the *Kodukan*, I will not end my study without reasonable cause; I will not dishonour the *dojo*; unless I am given permission, I will not disclose the secrets that I have been taught; unless I am given permission, I will not teach judo; pupil first, teacher second, I will always follow the rules of the *dojo*."

Demonstrating the dynamic throws in judo.

Close quarter gripping in preparation to throw or defend.

Competition

Judo today is one of the most wide-spread martial arts in the world, with reputedly more than 8 million students. Practitioners are referred to as *judoka* and competitions (*shiai*) are conducted under the supervision of a referee and judge. Contests and training take place in the *judojo* (hall). Free-style combat in judo is known as *randori*; the submitting opponent is known as the *uke*; and the winning partner is referred to as the *tori* in judo.

More than just sport

Judo is not purely about physical skill. Its aim is to teach good attitude and behaviour and to instil a sense of decorum in its *judoka*: best summed up in two terms used to describe the mental attitude expected from a *judoka*: *hontai*, demonstrating the state of permanent alertness and *bonno*, demonstrating a disciplined mind, serene and calm, controlling the body and being able to react to any situation.

Judo is suitable for people of all ages and abilities and is one of the more popular martial arts.

"Judo is the means of understanding the way to make the most effective use of both physical and spiritual power and strength. By devoted practice and rigid discipline, in an effort to obtain perfection in attacking and defending, it refines the body and soul and helps instil the spiritual essence in judo into every part of one's very being. In this way, it is possible to perfect oneself and contribute something worthwhile to the world." JIGURO KANO

BENEFITS OF JUDO

Judo is suitable for people of all ages and abilities, and the benefits to be derived from it affect many aspects of your everyday life. These include:

- Health, fitness and stamina
- Confidence and well-being
- Self-defence skills
- Comradeship
- Flexibility and agility
- Awareness and assertiveness
- Strengthened limbs

Demonstrating the skill of break-falling.

It is very important that the training area is always kept clean and tidy. Ideally the floor should be swept before practice and usually the first student to arrive would undertake this responsibility. Any cause for concern, such as holes or chips in the floor area, must be noted and avoided. All practitioners must be aware of both emergency exits and emergency procedures e.g. local hospital number, emergency number and escape route. The first aid kit must always be available in the dojo.

clothing *and*
equipment

A judo practitioner, a *judoka*, wears a *judogi*
consists of a heavy cotton jacket and tro
made of strong material so that it can with
the many grabs and tugs delivered in th
"way of gentleness" (Jiguro Kano 1860–
The word judo is based on jikishin-ryu
jitsu. Jiguro Kano wanted to turn ju-jitsu
a "martial sport" to train and educate you
people. Kano said "the aim of Judo is to
understand and demonstrate the living
laws of movement".

The techniques which upset an
opponent's balance and/or immobilize
him or her is known as *kuzushi*. The
main aim of judo is to neutralize an
opponent as opposed to injure or kill.
It is very much viewed as a self-
defence system.

Judoka train with bare feet on the
matted (*tatami*) area.

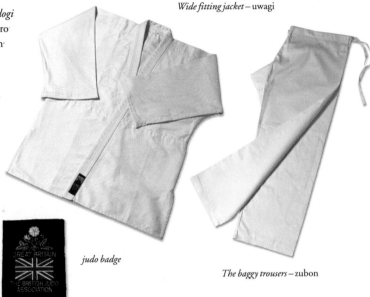

Wide fitting jacket – uwagi

judo badge

The baggy trousers – zubon

BELT GRADINGS	
9th-*kyu*	Yellow
7th–8th-*kyu*	Orange
5th–6th-*kyu*	Green
3rd–4th-*kyu*	Blue
1st–2nd-*kyu*	Brown
1st–5th-*dan*	Black
6th–7th-*dan*	Red and white
8th–10th-*dan*	Red

All beginners wear a white belt and there is a different belt
sequence for junior practitioners.

white belt

yellow belt

orange belt

green belt

blue belt

black belt

red/white belt

red belt

Etiquette

Etiquette and discipline are of the utmost importance in judo, not only to maintain respect and courtesy for the art and your opponent, but also to ensure safety. All practitioners must look after their personal appearance – especially their nails, which can scratch if they are too long or ragged.

❶ ◁ Stand upright and relaxed, with your eyes looking forwards and your feet a shoulder-width apart.

❷ ▷ Perform the bow by inclining your body by about 30 degrees. Let your eyes follow the bow to the floor, since this is given as a sign of respect to the art, the training environment and your fellow practitioners.

❸ ▷ When practising or in competition with a partner, the same bow is performed. It is important to allow adequate space between yourself and your partner to avoid bumping heads! Ideally, you need to be at approximately one and a half arms distance, as this maintains a safe personal boundary. In competition, you take one step back and then bow to your partner.

Exercise | Warm-up

The idea behind this exercise routine is to loosen the whole of your body, making your muscles and joints as flexible as possible, in order to prevent injuries during training. What is unique to judo is the emphasis on preparing the body for grappling and throwing moves. A general warm-up must be carried out first, in preparation for the actual techniques.

WARM-UP 1 – *Sit-ups help to develop stomach muscles and stamina. Be careful to build this exercise up gradually to avoid injury.*

◁ Lie flat on the floor. Bend your knees at approximately 90 degrees, never straight, with your partner holding your ankles. Place your hands at the sides of your head. The tips of your fingers should be in the region of your temples. Keep your elbows tucked in and raise your body about 45 degrees from the floor as you exhale. Then lower yourself down as you inhale. Repeat this exercise several times.

WARM-UP 2 – *The star jump assists in the overall body warm-up process and builds stamina.*

❶ ◁ For the star jump, stand in a relaxed, natural position, feet a shoulder-width apart, and hands at your sides.

❷ ▷ Jump into an X position – legs spread and arms raised – and then back into the standing position. Repeat this about ten times.

WARM-UP 3 – *Press-ups (push-ups) assist in developing the upper part of the body. Take your time and build up gradually and carefully.*

◁ Lie face down on the floor, with your legs slightly apart. Make sure you are on the balls of your feet and place your hands approximately in line with your shoulders. Slowly inhale as you raise your body upwards. Keep your body level and arms straight. Gently lower yourself, just touching the floor, but do not take the weight off your arms. Build up to sets of 10 if possible.

WARM-UP 4 – *Leg stretches, such as this inner-thigh stretch, are important as part of your preparation for judo practice.*

◁ Sit on the floor with legs spread as far as possible. Lower your upper body as far as you comfortably can, towards your left knee. Keep your leg straight and aim to go a little further down each time you practise. Don't worry if you cannot manage this in the early stages: it takes time to become supple. Repeat 10 times to the left side and then the right side, holding for approximately 10 seconds.

WARM-UP 5 (*UCHI-KOME*) – *An important part of the warm-up routine is preparation for throwing.*

❶ △ Face your partner and take hold of his right sleeve with your left hand. Your partner takes hold of your left lapel with his right hand. *Note: this technique is also performed to the opposite side e.g. left and right grabs.*

❷ △ As you move, step through with your right foot and bring your right arm under your partner's left arm.

❸ △ Rotate your body around until your back makes contact with your partner's front and your feet are in-between your partner's, with you legs slightly bent. Push your right hip back towards your partner and gently pull him forwards and downwards over your right shoulder. Remember, this is only an exercise, so don't carry the throw through. Return to the start position and repeat the exercise several times.

Technique | Basic throws

Throwing techniques form the basis of judo, aiming to disrupt the partner's point of balance, and therefore do not rely on strength, but on skill and good timing. Professional supervision is vitally important when practising all throws. The following techniques are only a guide to some of those used and are performed from both right and left grabs.

BODY DROP (*TIA-OTOSHI*) – *Disrupting the partner's point of balance in preparation to throw.*

❶△ Stand facing your partner. Grab your partner's lapel with your right hand and her sleeve with your left hand. Your partner also takes hold of your lapel with her right hand and your left arm with her left hand.

❷△ Step forwards with your right leg, turning your right shoulder in towards your partner. Keep an upright posture and maintain a secure grip of your partner's clothing in preparation for the throwing technique.

❸△ Lower your stance to maintain good posture and balance, and use your body momentum to throw your partner.

HOOKING TECHNIQUE (*KO-UCHI GARI*) – *A smaller person can overcome a larger person.*

SWEEPING TECHNIQUE (*ASHI WAZA*)

❶△ Your left arm is grabbed, above the elbow, by your partner. Move in close.

❷△ Hook the inside of his right leg, and use your momentum to throw your partner backwards and downwards.

❸◁ Project your body forwards and throw him to the floor.

△ A popular technique in judo is the "sweep". The aim is to catch your partner's lower leg/foot with a scooping action as they move forwards, using the inside of your foot in an outwards and inwards motion. At the same time, grab your partner's clothing. Both partners must be well versed in break-falling and beginners must have qualified supervision.

Technique | Floor restraint

Following a take down to the floor, a variety of restraints can be applied. When correctly performed, a partner can be kept restrained for some time. In competition, the partner has to be held for 25 seconds to qualify for any point(s). The following techniques would be applied to gain points if a throw has not been won.

△ After throwing your partner, pin her down by lying across her chest. Your right arm should be positioned around her right leg and your left arm around the back of her neck. Take hold of your partner's clothing where it is accessible. Spread your legs well apart to give good balance and to increase the pressure on your partner's body.

❶ ▷ If you are being attacked while sitting on the floor, control your partner with your legs and secure her head with your arms. Now turn her on to her back. Move through with your left arm in preparation for securing your partner and turning her towards the floor.

❷ ▽ Once you have turned your partner towards the floor, secure her by applying an upper body hold.

CAUTION
It is important to ensure that your partner's windpipe is not smothered by your restraint, so that they can breathe freely and advise you of any possible discomfort. This is particularly important in training where a technique is being demonstrated by an adult against a junior. Some techniques are not allowed to be practised on young people under the age of 16, particularly choking techniques.

Technique | Defence tactics

There are a variety of self-defence moves in judo which equip a student to deal with attacks from different angles. The following demonstrates a defensive move from a rear attack, using the opponent's body weight to their disadvantage. In judo, you learn to overcome your opponent's attack by displacing their centre of gravity.

SELF-DEFENCE 1

1 ◁ An aggressor grabs you around the neck from the rear, with his right arm placed across your throat.

2 ◁ Take hold of the aggressor's right sleeve and push your hips back into his body. At the same time, pull his right arm over your shoulder in a forward and downward action. Bend your legs and rotate your body so that you can throw your partner.

◁ This side view shows the same movement, and you can clearly see how projecting your hips backwards unbalances the aggressor. This demonstrates how to move into the aggressor's centre of gravity to break their point of balance. It also reveals how a smaller individual can overcome a larger person.

3 △ Keep the momentum going so that your opponent is thrown over your shoulder and on to the floor. The force of the throw should incapacitate him, giving you time to get to a safe place.

1 △ An aggressor is coming at you from the front and grabs the clothing on either side of your neck.

2 △ Place your hand under your partner's chin. Step forwards and sweep away the legs.

3 △ Maintain the pressure under his chin in order to break his balance.

4 △ Keep the momentum going and throw the aggressor to the floor.

TECHNIQUE JUDO

▷ This side view of step 4 shows the hand grip in more detail.

Technique | Choke and strangle

This section demonstrates a variety of choke and strangle techniques. A choke is defined as putting pressure against the windpipe; a strangle is pressure against the blood supply, such as the jugular vein. These are highly-skilled techniques and the intention is to learn these as a means of developing advanced skills only.

CAUTION

These techniques are advanced moves developed for the purpose of restraining in a self-defence situation. They are very specialized and must be practised under strict supervision. Young people under 16 years old, in particular, must not practise certain moves, or have such techniques applied to them.

HADAKA-JIME

▽ The *hadaka-jime* is a choke technique in which the forearm is locked against the windpipe. It is important to keep your body close with feet astride to maintain control.

△ Place your forearm against your partner's windpipe and pull him towards you, forcing the head forward. Keep your hands well clasped together and secure your head close to your partner's. Any gaps will allow your partner to escape.

OKURI-ERI-JIME

▽ In this basic strangle technique (*okuri-eri-jime*), pressure is applied to the side of the neck, cutting the blood supply, as opposed to the air supply.

Technique | Leg and arm locks

Here *juji-gatame* (straight-arm lock) and *ude-garame* (bent-arm lock) are demonstrated. *Juji-garame* is a complex groundwork technique which involves using both your arms and legs. The pressure that is applied by this technique restricts your opponent's ability to break free even when the arms and legs have limited movement.

JUJI-GATAME
▷ By pinning the opponent in this position, their body is immobilized by the straight-arm lock. Pull the arm across your body and lift your hips in order to apply pressure to the extended straight arm.

UDE-GARAME
▽ Take a figure 4 position with your arms and bend your opponent's arms upwards by pressing downwards on their wrist.

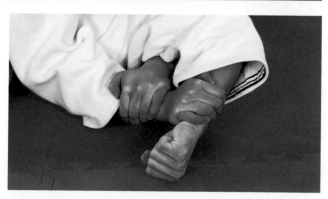

▷ There are several variations of this technique, namely a straight-arm lock (*juji-gatame*) and a bent-arm lock (*ude-garame*). *Ude-garame* is shown demonstrating the bent-arm lock as part of a floor restraining technique. *Note: you should be lying across your opponent with your legs splayed, to maintain body pressure.*

index

A
aikido, 48–79
  back-stretching, 62–5
  breathing, 61
  clothing and equipment, 54
  cool-down exercises, 78–9
  etiquette, 55
  history, 50–3
  spiritual development, 60
  techniques, 66–77
  warm-up exercises, 56–9
  weapons, 77
arm locks, judo, 127
arm pinning, aikido, 68–9

B
back-stretching, aikido, 62–5
belt grading see grading
blocking: ju-jitsu, 92–3
  shotokan, 42, 44–5
  wado ryu, 31
bo, 110
bow: aikido, 55
  ju-jitsu, 87
  judo, 119
  shotokan, 37
  wado ryu, 18–19
breathing, aikido, 61
bushido, 84

C
choke techniques, judo, 126
clothes: aikido, 54
  ju-jitsu, 85–6
  judo, 118
  shotokan, 36
  wado ryu, 16–17
competitions: judo, 116
  karate, 13
cool-down exercises, aikido, 78–9

D
defence: aikido, 67, 72–5
  ju-jitsu, 96-101, 104–7
  judo, 124–5
  shotokan, 42
  wado ryu, 32

E
elbow restraint, ju-jitsu, 100
elbow strike, shotokan, 46–7
equipment: aikido, 54
  ju-jitsu, 86
  wado ryu, 16
etiquette: aikido, 55
  ju-jitsu, 87
  judo, 119
  shotokan, 37
  wado ryu, 18–19

F
floor restraint, judo, 123
Funakoshi, Gichin, 12, 14, 34, 35
Funakoshi, Yoshitaka, 34

G
grading: aikido, 52–3
  ju-jitsu, 85
  judo, 118
  shotokan, 36
  wado ryu, 16
guard position, shotokan, 41

H
history: aikido, 50–3
  ju-jitsu, 82–4
  judo, 114–16
  karate, 10–13
  shotokan, 34–5
  wado ryu, 14–15
hojo jutsu, 111

I
ikkyo, 68

J
jo, 111
ju-jitsu, 80–111
  clothing and equipment, 85–6
  etiquette, 87
  history, 82–4
  techniques, 92–111
  warm-up exercises, 88–91
  weapons, 108–11
judo, 112–27
  clothing, 118
  etiquette, 119
  history, 114–16
  techniques, 122–7
  warm-up exercises, 120–1

K
kamma, 108
Kanazawa, Hirokazu, 34
Kano, Jiguro, 114–15
kata, 13, 22–9
kata dori, 70–1
kicking, shotokan, 43
kneeling techniques, aikido, 58
knife defence: aikido, 75
  ju-jitsu, 104–6
kotegaeshi, 69
kumite, 13, 30

L
leg locks, judo, 127

M
meditation, 19

N
nage waga, 76
neck, loosening, 58
neck lock, 31

O
Ohtsuka, Hironori, 15
Ohtsuka, Jiro, 15
otagani rei, 37

P
passive defensive stance,
  ju-jitsu, 96–7
pinan nidan, 22–9
posture, aikido, 66

R
rear defence, aikido, 72
rear stranglehold, defence from, 101
rei see bow

S
sai, 109
samurai, 84
search technique, ju-jitsu, 102–3
self-defence see defence
shotokan, 34–47
  clothing, 36
  etiquette, 37
  history, 34–5
  techniques, 40–7
  warm-up exercises, 38–9
shoulder lock, ju-jitsu, 94–5
soto uke block, shotokan, 44–5, 46
spiritual development, aikido, 60
stance: aikido, 66
  ju-jitsu, 96–7
strangle techniques, judo, 126
suwari-waza, 68

T
taisabaki, 33
Takeda, Sokaku, 50
tanto-jutsu, 111
throws: aikido, 76
  judo, 122
tonfa, 110
triads, 34–5
two-person exercises, wado ryu, 30

U
Ueshiba, Morihei, 50

W
wado ryu, 14–33
  defence, 32
  history, 14–15
  taisabaki, 33
  two-person exercises, 30
  warm-up exercises: aikido, 56–9
  ju-jitsu, 88–91
  judo, 120–1
  shotokan, 38–9
  wado ryu, 20–1
weapons: aikido, 77
  ju-jitsu, 108–11
women, self-defence, 74
wrist defence, ju-jitsu, 98–9
wrist flexibility, 59
wrist locks, shotokan, 46–7

Y
yin and yang, 50–51

ACKNOWLEDGEMENTS
The support and help of the following
is acknowledged with gratitude:

Eugene Codrington and his team,
Father Seamus Mulholland and
Juliette, Graham Kenning, Hiroshi
Sugawara, James Sinclair and his team,
Kerstie Hodrien, Kerry Elkins, Kevin
Pell and Miguel Camacho, Mark
Wolski, Neil Adams and his team, Paul
Boyer and Chris Goodburn, Peter
Brady, Cath Davies, Ron Sergiew and
his team, Roy Preece and family,
Robert Poyton and his team, David
Mills of CIMAC, Haruna Matsuo
Sensei, Ishido Shizufumi Sensei,
Oshita Masakaza Sensei, Fujji
Okimitsu Sensei, Fukura Sensei, Ide
Sensei, Chiba Sensei, Kanetsuka
Sensei, Hirori Sensei, Eddie Daniels, A
Hunt and T Forster.

MODEL ACKNOWLEDGEMENTS:
wado ryu: Simon Walker *shotokan:*
Juliette Littlewood *aikido:* Cath
Davies *ju-jitsu:* Miguel Camacho
judo: Ceri Richards, Emma George,
Andy Smith and Ashley Adams.

PICTURE CREDITS – Additional
pictures supplied by:
Hulton Getty: p12 top, p15 top,
p82, p84 left, p114.
Tony Stone: p6 top, p7 bottom, p11,
p13, p51, p83, p115 top.
Simon Lailey: p10, p12 bottom, p14,
p34, p35 both.
e.t. archive: p51, p83.

**FOR GENERAL ENQUIRIES REGARDING
MARTIAL ARTS:**
www.masamune.co.uk

INDEX

128

INDEX